RETURN ON INVESTMENT
Strategies for Profit

Robert Rachlin

A SPECTRUM BOOK

PRENTICE-HALL, INC., *Englewood Cliffs, New Jersey 07632*

HG
4028
C4
R255
1978

Library of Congress Cataloging in Publication Data

Rachlin, Robert, (date)
  Return on investment.

  (A Spectrum Book)
  Includes index.
  1. Capital investments—Evaluation. 2. Corporations
  —Finance. I. Title.
  HG4028.C4R255 1978   658.1'55   78-26945
  ISBN 0-13-779116-X
  ISBN 0-13-779108-9 pbk.

Dedicated to my wife Roseann
and my children Melinda and Amy

A SPECTRUM BOOK

10   9   8   7   6   5   4   3   2   1

Printed in the United States of America

PRENTICE-HALL INTERNATIONAL, INC., *London*

PRENTICE-HALL OF AUSTRALIA PTY. LIMITED, *Sydney*

PRENTICE-HALL OF CANADA, LTD., *Toronto*

PRENTICE-HALL OF INDIA PRIVATE LIMITED, *New Delhi*

PRENTICE-HALL OF JAPAN, INC., *Tokyo*

PRENTICE-HALL OF SOUTHEAST ASIA PTE. LTD., *Singapore*

WHITEHALL BOOKS LIMITED, *Wellington, New Zealand*

CONTENTS

ROBERT RACHLIN is a recognized authority on return-on-investment concepts and applications and is a financial consultant to several leading corporations in the country. He has served as New York Chapter President of the Planning Executives Institute.

CHAPTER 1

INTRODUCTION

For most companies, probably no other area of decision making is as important to its success as resource utilization and evaluation. Management is constantly faced with a wide array of possible resource investment alternatives and is responsible for the funds entrusted to its care. The selection of the most profitable alternative, recognizing the availability of funds and resources required to finance the investment, can be considered a major function of management.

The primary objective of the financial manager is to utilize funds of the company within the limits of his authority, so that over the long run, the company receives at least as high a rate of return on its investment as might be obtained in alternative investments of similar risk. The second most important objective is the maximization of the present value of resource investments to obtain as high a return as possible without assuming undue risks. To maximize the earning power of the company, resources are allocated in such a way that the earning power will be converted into as high a rate of return as possible for the company. To accomplish these objectives, measures are needed to appraise company performance. One basic measure is return-on-investment which describes the relationships between earnings and investment.

It is assumed that a business has a prime objective of generating an adequate return to the owner's. Recognizing that there may be other objectives, we must make the above statement since we are going to explore different techniques of measuring financial performance. In the course of discussion, it will be pointed out that it is necessary to reduce as many of the intuitive factors of decision making to a more systematic and mathematical approach. However, it is important to recognize that return-on-investment concepts will never replace sound business judgments, but rather, aid in supporting or raising questions as to the validity of these business judgment factors. It is what it is intended to be, a financial management tool which defines the problem, evaluates and weighs possible alternative investments, and brings into focus those qualitative factors affecting the decision which may not be expressed in quantitative terms.

Why is Return-on-Investment Important

Return-on-investment is important because it aids in maintaining a company's growth by measuring historical results and assists in the evaluation of anticipated future performance. It is also important because of the acceptability of the technique by investors, the business community, the financial community, economists, and most students of business concepts. With this kind of recognition, and the fact that ROI can provide a technique for evaluating alternatives for changing a company's relative attractiveness to the concerned community, it is easy to see why ROI is so important.

Why Use Return-on-Investment

In today's complex business environment, technological, economic, and competitive pressures tend to complicate managerial decision making. This management tool provides management with an easy method of evaluating and communicating, both past and anticipated future performance, more effectively, in an effort to increase growth as well as productivity. The following highlights why ROI is recommended and what the concept may do in enhancing the decision making process.

- *It forces planning* – corporate management must have a plan, whether it be short-term or long-term, in order to measure efficiency and to set goals.
- *As a basis for decision making* – it takes certain decisions out of the realm of intuition into the realm of supportive and quantitative basis.
- *To evaluate investment opportunities* – this can include not only initial capital investments, but also the cost of additional working capital, the economic life of the investment, and the effect on company profitability. These investment opportunities will also include alternative investments or new product opportunities.
- *Aid in evaluating management performance* – this would include performance of responsibility or profit center heads, as well as total company performance against a common denominator, or against planned measures of performance or predetermined objectives. It aids in eliminating inequities which might arise between managers or operating units due to differences in size and make-up of operations, i.e., highly intensified capital operations vs. distributive operations which may have very little capital investment. In addition, per-

formance measurement can be used to evaluate management's use of assets, cash flow, capital, equipment or other facilities, and internal control.

- *Response to marketplace* – measures management's response to changes in the marketplace on pricing and need, as well as profitability and cost reduction measures.

Understanding the Definition

To understand ROI, it is necessary to review the term itself. A great deal of confusion sometimes arises as to the term ROI. The word "return on" refers to an additional sum of money expected from an investment over and above the original investment. This return may be before or after taxes. An investment may be defined as the employment of an economic resource such as money, machinery and equipment, manpower, etc., with the anticipation of producing a gain either in the form of income, appreciated value, greater efficiency, or cost savings. This gain is measured over a period of time. Therefore, return-on-investment measures gain on economic resources over a period of time usually in the form of a ratio.

Management's Need for Involvement

Management's involvement is required since justification of any investment opportunity is directly related to the participation of persons with both technical knowledge and the expertise to recognize the relationship of all input data. This also serves as an integral part of training and the development of manager skills. Management must recognize that the development of profitable investment opportunities frequently start at the lower levels of management by both technical and non-technical personnel. In addition, management aids in establishing the areas of responsibility as well as the level of authority.

Major Uses and Applications

While the list of uses and applications can be quite extensive, it is important to identify the major applications. Most of these will be discussed in greater detail later in the text. It is important to note that in the later discussions of these applications, a company must evaluate which application and/or techniques best serves their needs.

- *External measurement* — a comparative technique of comparing ROI calculations to other companies and industries.

- *Internal measurement* — a technique of evaluating internal segments of a company resulting in increased earnings contribution through cost reduction and/or profit improvement.

- *Improving asset utilization* — ways of improving the utilization of cash, inventories, receivables, and capital assets for greater profitability.

- *Capital expenditure evaluation* — most recognized techniques for providing the tools for effectively allocating capital resources.

- *Divestments* — used to reflect the impact of divesting businesses or segments for improving ROI.

- *Profit goals* — through internal and external measurements, a company's profit goals can be established.

- *Acquisitions* — measures the impact of acquisitions on the short and long-term growth of the company.

- *Management incentives* — technique of rewarding incentives based on ROI performance measurements.

- *Elimination or addition to product lines* — techniques can strengthen the focus on profitable or unprofitable existing or new product lines.

- *Make or buy decisions* — measurement of the ROI impact for making or buying a product.

- *Lease or purchase decision* — similar to capital expenditures evaluation techniques used in comparing lease vs. purchase decisions of acquiring capital assets.

- *Evaluating human resources* — this concept is still in the early stages of development, but determining the return on people may have an application.

- *Inventory control* — measures the incremental changes of inventory and earnings generated from that additional inventory investment.

- *Pricing* — guide in developing the price of a product using the desired rate of return. This would include intercompany pricing.

Understanding the Concept

The ROI as previously explored, measures historical and anticipated future earnings. Within each category, i.e., past vs. future, different methods and techniques are applied for different decisions necessary to manage the business. Keep in mind, that within each of the categories, many variations can be computed.

HISTORICAL	FUTURE
Performance Measurement	Capital Evaluation
through	through
Return on Capital Employed	Payback Methods
Return on Total Assets	Accounting Methods
Return on Controllable Assets	Discounted Cash Flow Methods
for	for
Internal Measurement	Improving Asset Utilization
External Measurement	Capital Expenditure Evaluations
Distributive Channels	Divestments and Acquisitions
Incentives	Setting of Profit Goals
Pricing	Lease vs. Purchase Decisions
Product Reviews	Make or Buy Decisions

While these are but some of the uses and techniques for the ROI concept, they nevertheless highlight the need for integrating all segments into an overall company objective.

Cautions in Using Concept

The use of return-on-investment techniques in evaluating external and internal performance as a tool for management decision making, should be used with caution. Like all methods of evaluation, improper interpretation can arise out of measuring different sets of comparative data by relying too heavily upon a single measurement device. The tool of return-on-investment is a vital management tool, but certain cautions must be recognized in its use.

Too often, managers make decisions by comparing absolute relationships between sets of data, without giving consideration to the meaningful relationship to the components of the data. This misconception can lead to wrong decisions, unless further interpretations are given to the meaning of the results. Therefore, the first caution to consider in ROI, is not to rely exclusively on the absolute numerical results in calculating ROI rates, whether it is between products, departments, divisions, companies, or industries. Such areas of operations as the nature of comparative products, quality of products, nature of selling, production costs, corporate structure, are but some of the areas to be considered before reaching any sound conclusions.

The rule of consistency is perhaps one of the most important cautions that can be mentioned. This rule will continuously be referred to, since it is the basis to which the concept of ROI is conceived. The rule of consistency is important if you understand how ROI functions. Since ROI measures comparative data over a period of time, it is important to be consistent in measuring like data. Once a method of comparison is chosen, the ground rules must remain consistent. For example, if comparisons are calculated using certain allocations, this must continually be used in future comparisons if any valid conclusions are to be reached. If the ground rules change, both historical and future calculations must be changed to develop an accurate trend of operations. This rule would hold true for all comparisons of data and is most important in measuring ROI. Remember, consistency must be adhered to if accurate decisions are to be reached. ROI is only the tool to aid in reaching these decisions, and not the ultimate solution.

Failure to use other supporting measures of performance can put too much emphasis on ROI as a management tool. Other sound methods of evaluations should be used to support conclusions reached through ROI calculations, such as growth rates, and other techniques and processes found in the budgeting and planning aspects of a company's short and long-range planning. These processes along with ROI, will provide a sound and intelligent basis for appraising performance in both the short and long-run.

Allocating Components

It is important to properly assign the net sales, net earnings and investment into segments for evaluating performance. These segments can be divisions, product lines, departments, accountability centers, marketing segments, etc. The question arises as to whether all data should be allocated, or whether only data for which a manager has responsibility and authority should be used. Let's address ourselves to that problem.

If you accept the rule of consistency, it doesn't matter whether you allocate, as long as you are consistent in measuring like data from period to period. The ultimate return-on-investment rate can be adjusted upward, if lower investments are allocated, and adjusted downward if higher investments are assigned to the segment. Therefore, it appears that the more likely approach should be taken which measures performance in accordance with what a manager is responsible for and what authority a manager is given. It is recommended that only data which can be identified as controllable by a manager be used. Other data which may be allocated and not under a manager's authority, could lead to erroneous decisions and force an operating segment into decisions detrimental to the operation, i.e., increasing prices to meet ROI objectives. The other unassigned data can be used to complete the entire company's operation in the establishment of overall goals. For example, the following format can be used in determining controllable return-on-investment by segment and the relationship to the overall company.

Controllable Data

	Net Sales	Net Earnings	Investment	Return-on-Investment
Operation A	xxx	xxx	xxx	x
Operation B	xxx	xxx	xxx	x
Operation C	xxx	xxx	xxx	x
Operation D	xxx	xxx	xxx	x
Total Controllable	xxx	xxx	xxx	x
Uncontrollable Data				
Other Sales	xxx	xxx		
Other Expenses		xxx		
Corporate Overhead		xxx		
Taxes		xxx		
Other Investments			xxx	
Total Company	xxx	xxx	xxx	x

You can see that each operation can be measured on those components which are controllable by a manager. Each operation is given an ROI objective and should coincide with the overall objective after other uncontrollable data is included.

It is suggested that earnings before taxes be used on the controllable components, and net earnings on the overall company. Since taxes are difficult to compute on individual segments, only net earnings should be used for overall evaluation. In addition, it is recommended that for short evaluation periods, i.e., less than one year, period-end balances be used for the investment base. For longer periods, i.e., one year or longer, year-end balances should be used for the investment base or a variation of the average of the beginning and closing yearly balances, moving averages, or any other variation. The conclusion will not alter as long as consistency is followed. Remember, the absolute rates are not as important as is the incremental changes that occur from period to period. This indicates the performance trend, and will act as an indicator of performance in the past, as well as the future.

Net sales and net earnings should be accumulated for each period such as three months year-to-date for a quarter of a year, six months year-to-date for a half of a year, etc. No averaging of balances are necessary for net sales and net earnings, since they are not balances at any given period in time like the balance sheet, but performance data after each period of operations and can be accumulated for any given period desired.

CHAPTER 2

RATIOS

It is important to understand financial ratios, since they provide some answers and possible solutions in highlighting the position and/or trend of a company's performance. In addition, it is the basis for computing ROI calculations, since in most cases, a numerator and denominator will be used in arriving at a decision. Since we established that ROI was a financial tool, it is logical to conclude that items of evaluation may be selected from the earnings statement and/or balance sheet. In addition, since the complexity of both the earnings statement and balance sheet exists, hundreds of ratios can be developed. It is not the purpose of this chapter to develop all these possible ratios, but rather to highlight and set the stage for other ratios so commonly used in ROI.

It appears that reviewing the selection of ratios presented for evaluating management performance, ratios can be developed for varying levels of activity within a company. This is not to say that all ratios can be assigned to a specific level of activity within a company, but it seems to fit a very close pattern, whereby ratios can be considered like an organizational chart in developing the hierarchy of financial responsibility. For example, as the pyramid narrows in the organization chart, management becomes more concerned with the overall performance of the company, and less with the day-to-day routine of running the business. Priorities differ, and responsibilities differ, but ultimate objectives remain the same. Greater productivity and ultimately, greater profits. Within each level of responsibility, a different ROI ratio assumes a different role. It is under this assumption, that ratios can be broken down into three basic levels of ratio activity. They are performance ratios, managing ratios, and profitability ratios. Remember, these ratios are only guidelines in providing facts for interpretation, and also the basis for further analysis within a company and/or industry. The following earnings statement and balance sheet will be used for all calculations.

Earnings Statement

Net Sales		$1,500,000
Cost of goods sold		1,250,000
Gross profit		250,000
Less operating expenses:		
Selling expenses	$30,000	
General expenses	15,000	
Administrative expenses	10,000	55,000
Gross operating income		195,000
Depreciation		20,000
Net operating income		175,000
Other income		10,000
Other expense		5,000
Net before income tax		180,000
Income tax		90,000
Net earnings		$ 90,000

Balance Sheet

Assets

Cash	$ 30,000
Marketable securities	70,000
Receivables — net	120,000
Inventories	180,000
Total current assets	400,000
Gross plant and equipment	600,000
Less depreciation	100,000
Net plant and equipment	500,000
Total Assets	$900,000

Liabilities

Accounts payable	$ 50,000
Notes payable	70,000
Accruals	10,000
Provision for federal income taxes	70,000
Total current liabilities	200,000
Long-term debt	250,000
Preferred stockholders' equity	100,000
Common stockholders' equity	150,000
Paid-in surplus	50,000
Retained earnings	150,000

| Total net worth | 450,000 |
| Total liabilities | $900,000 |

Performance Ratios

These ratios review the overall performance of a company and is viewed by the outside community as a way of measuring current and potential performance. Some of these ratios are as follows:

Net Earnings to Net Worth – indicates how well the owners' capital is being employed in the business.

$$\frac{\text{Net Earnings}}{\text{Net Worth}} = \frac{\$90,000}{\$450,000} = 20\%$$

Net Earnings to Total Assets – represents the return on funds invested in the company by both owners and creditors.

$$\frac{\text{Net Earnings}}{\text{Total Assets}} = \frac{\$90,000}{\$900,000} = 10\%$$

Managing Ratios

These ratios evaluate the various items of the balance sheet and is used to manage such major areas of the company as cash, inventories, receivables, and debt relationships.

Current Ratio – a general indication of the ability of the company (borrower) to meet its current obligations.

$$\frac{\text{Current Assets}}{\text{Current Liabilities}} = \frac{\$400,000}{\$200,000} = 2.0 \text{ times}$$

Acid Test Ratio – a supplement to the current ratio in measuring liquidity and the ability of a company to meet current obligations by placing emphasis on those liquid assets which can be quickly converted into cash, namely, cash, marketable securities, and receivables (quick assets).

$$\frac{\text{Cash, Marketable Securities and Receivables}}{\text{Current Liabilities}} = \frac{\$220,000}{\$200,000} = 1.1 \text{ times}$$

Debt-Equity Ratio – indicates the extent to which a company is financed by borrowed capital and the extent to which a company is financed by permanent contributed capital.

Long-Term Debt	$250,000	35.7%
Stockholders' Equity	450,000	64.3
Total	$700,000	100.0%

Day's Sales Outstanding — an indication of the average age of net customer's accounts receivable, with the possibility of greater past due accounts as the number of days sales outstanding increases.

$$\frac{\text{Net Annual Sales}}{360} = \frac{\$1,500,000}{360} = \$4,166.67 \text{ average daily sales}$$

$$\frac{\text{Receivables} - \text{Net}}{\text{Average Daily Sales}} = \frac{\$120,000}{\$4,166.67} = 28.8 \text{ days sales outstanding}$$

Sales to Receivables — an indication of the turnover of receivables during a year. As the ratio increases, the more rapid collection of sales is indicated.

$$\frac{\text{Net Sales}}{\text{Receivables} - \text{Net}} = \frac{\$1,500,000}{\$\ \ 120,000} = 12.5 \text{ times}$$

Inventory Turnover — indicates a company's turnover of inventory. As the ratio decreases, the greater the possibility the inventory is excessive and may include obsolete inventory.

$$\frac{\text{Cost of Goods Sold}}{\text{Inventories}} = \frac{\$1,250,000}{\$\ \ 180,000} = 6.9 \text{ times}$$

Day's Sales on Hand — indicates the average length in day's that inventories are held before sale.

$$\frac{\text{Cost of Goods Sold}}{360} = \frac{\$1,250,000}{360} = \$3,472.22 \text{ average daily cost of sales}$$

$$\frac{\text{Inventories}}{\substack{\text{Average Daily Cost} \\ \text{of Goods Sold}}} = \frac{\$180,000}{\$3,472.22} = 51.8 \text{ days sales on hand}$$

Net Sales to Net Working Capital — indicates the activity of net working capital.

$$\frac{\text{Net Sales}}{\text{Net Working Capital}} = \frac{\$1,500,000}{\$\ \ 200,000} = 7.5 \text{ times}$$

Profitability Ratios

These ratios relate to the earnings statement and the operations of each manager having operating responsibility.

Net Earnings to Net Sales — measures the profitability of sales.

$$\frac{\text{Net Earnings}}{\text{Net Sales}} = \frac{\$\ \ 90,000}{\$1,500,000} = 6\%$$

Gross Profit to Net Sales — indicates the margin of sales over the cost of goods sold.

$$\frac{\text{Gross Profit}}{\text{Net Sales}} = \frac{\$\ \ 250,000}{\$1,500,000} = 16.7\%$$

Selling Expenses to Net Sales — indicates the cost of selling a product.

$$\frac{\text{Selling Expenses}}{\text{Net Sales}} = \frac{\$\ \ 30,000}{\$1,500,000} = 2\%$$

In summary, these ratios are only financial guides and should be used with other evaluation techniques for measuring management performance.

CHAPTER 3

RELATIONSHIP BETWEEN ROI
AND THE ORGANIZATION

In the previous chapter, it was suggested that ratios could fit into an organization chart within each specific responsibility. This concept will be explored by presenting an organization chart using the Return on Capital Employed concept. Before this is done, it is important to explore the components of return-on-investment, and the relationship to the overall company.

Elements of Return-on-Investment

Return-on-investment derives its source data from the two most commonly used financial statements, namely, the Earnings Statement and the Balance Sheet. These have been previously presented in illustrating various ratio calculations. ROI is nothing more than a series of ratios in a logical sequence, in an effort to develop management decisions based on past and anticipated earnings, and asset utilization. With this in mind, it will be illustrated that ROI can be broken down into two basic components, using three different sets of data from the Earnings Statement and the Balance Sheet. These components are the Profitability Rate and the Turnover Rate.

Profitability Rate

The profitability rate is computed by dividing net sales into net earnings $\left(\dfrac{\text{net earnings}}{\text{net sales}} \right)$. This ratio highlights the relationship of how much earnings are generated from a sales dollar and measures the success in the controlling of costs. This is a familiar ratio in most businesses, and plays a major role in operating the business. For example, you will see that this ratio has the greatest leverage in generating higher returns for a company. This is possible, since when sales decline, most companies will experience lower earnings. To offset these lower sales dollars, expenses are generally reduced in order to maintain certain anticipated earnings. Therefore, immediate actions can be taken to compensate for temporary malfunctioning of the business. In our illustration, the profitability rate is as follows:

$$\frac{\text{Net Earnings}}{\text{Net Sales}} = \frac{\$90,000}{\$1,500,000} = 6\%$$

This means that six cents of every dollar of revenue results in a profit after tax.

Turnover Rate

The other component is the Turnover Rate and is computed by dividing the investment into the net sales $\left(\frac{\text{net sales}}{\text{investment}}\right)$ and is expressed as a rate. This turnover rate reflects the rapidity with which capital committed to an operation is being worked. The biggest problem of this ratio is determining what investment base to use, since the results will vary depending on the type of investment used. For example, using total assets the following turnover results:

$$\frac{\text{Net Sales}}{\text{Total Assets}} = \frac{\$1,500,000}{\$900,000} = 1.67 \text{ times}$$

or, using capital employed, the following results:

$$\frac{\text{Net Sales}}{\substack{\text{Total Assets} \\ \text{less} \\ \text{Current Liabilities}}} = \frac{\$1,500,000}{\$700,000} = 2.14 \text{ times}$$

The different types of investment bases can be many. However, whichever is determined, that base will assume the type of ROI used. For example, using total assets, ROI is referred to as Return on Total Assets. Using capital employed, ROI would be referred to as Return on Capital Employed. Therefore, the investment base will determine the technique used, since ROI measures the return on some investment base.

Relationship Between the Profitability Rate and Turnover Rate

Taking both the profitability rate and the turnover rate, the following results:

$$\frac{\text{Net Earnings}}{\text{Net Sales}} \quad X \quad \frac{\text{Net Sales}}{\text{Investment}}$$

Looking at the above components, you can see that the net sales in both equations can be cancelled resulting in the following:

$$\frac{\text{Net Earnings}}{\text{Investment}}$$

As pointed out previously, the reason the ratio is broken down into two components, is to review the relationship of earnings to sales and the rapidity to which committed capital is being used effectively. In addition, you can see that to improve the ROI rate, a manager can increase the profitability rate by increasing sales, reducing expenses, or a combination of the both. Also, the ROI rate can increase by working existing investments harder, thus, increasing the turnover rate. This is assumed that all these factors are under the control of the manager being measured. For example, let's assume that two managers have the responsibility for individual operations. The following facts are presented to illustrate the point.

	Manager A	**Manager B**
Net Sales	$1,500,000	$1,500,000
Net Earnings	90,000	120,000
Investment – Capital Employed	$ 700,000	$ 937,500
Profitability Rate	6%	8%
Turnover Rate	2.14	1.6
Return-on-Investment	12.86%	12.8%

You can see that both managers have the same sales dollars and the same ROI rate. Which manager is more effective? Without a detailed analysis of each operation, Manager B could be considered the better manager. This is due to the fact that Manager B generates greater flexibility in controlling the profitability rate, Manager B would be favored based on the above facts. However, caution should be taken to further analyze the details supporting Managers' B results in both financial and non-financial data.

Applying the profitability rate and the turnover rate, for Manager A, the following return on capital employed results:

Profitability Rate X   Turnover Rate

$$\frac{\text{Net Earnings}}{\text{Net Sales}} \quad X \quad \frac{\text{Net Sales}}{\text{Capital Employed}}$$

equals

$$\frac{\$ \quad 90,000}{\$1,500,000} \quad X \quad \frac{\$1,500,000}{\$ \quad 700,000}$$

or

$$6\% \quad X \quad 2.14$$

results in

12.86%

or

$$\frac{\$ \quad 90,000}{\$700,000} = 12.86\%$$

Organization Chart — Return on Capital Employed

The following organization chart of ROI responsibility is presented using Return on Capital Employed. Note that each function is assigned or contributes to the ultimate objective of return-on-investment. In this illustration, working capital (current assets less current liabilities) is used, plus fixed assets, resulting in the term capital employed. Other variations of the investment can be used, but the rule of consistency must be adhered to.

Industry Comparisons

External review and analysis is important to put into perspective a company's performance with that of its competitors, and the industry in total. Composites of similar companies are meaningful to the extent that it shows a company's relative position, and why a company may be favorable or unfavorable. Further analysis will be presented to show how this may be done in detail. However, utilizing the profitability rate and the turnover rate, can lead to some clues and possible answers, to a company's competitive position. The following illustrates this point.

You will note that competitor C has the highest profitability rate, but the lowest turnover rate. Company A has a profitability rate of 6%, which is four percentage points lower than competitor C, but is able to maintain a 1.67 turnover rate, which results in a 10% return on total assets. It is obvious that both com-

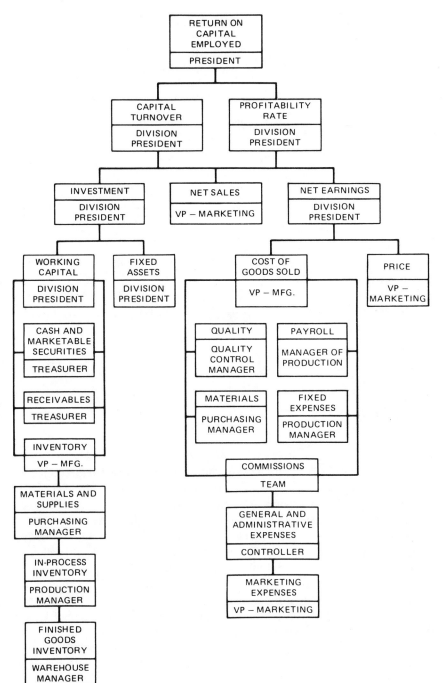

Competitive Relationship
of the
Profitability Rate
and the Turnover Rate

		Competitor	
	Company A	B	C
Profitability Rate			
Net Earnings	$ 90,000	$ 60,000	$ 100,000
divided by			
Net Sales	1,500,000	2,000,000	1,000,000
Profitability Rate	6%	3%	10%
Turnover Rate			
Net Sales	$1,500,000	$2,000,000	$1,000,000
divided by			
Total Assets	900,000	1,500,000	1,250,000
Turnover Rate	1.67	1.33	.80
Return on Total Assets			
Profitability Rate	6%	3%	10%
multiplied by			
Turnover Rate	1.67	1.33	.80
Return on Assets	10.0%	4.0%	8.0%

ponents must be further analyzed and caution given to such internal variations as differences in accounting policies, nature of the businesses, and overall general structure. However, as a point of reference, this provides an excellent opportunity to put into perspective a company's position relative to its competitors.

It is possible to develop a table of the profitability rate and the turnover rate at different levels of return-on-investment rates. For example, the following table illustrates the relationship of the profitability rate and the turnover rate at return-on-investment rates of 5% and 10%. Note that any combination of the profitability rate and the turnover rate will result in a specific return-on-investment. For example, at 10% return-on-investment, a profitability rate of 6% and a turnover rate of 1.67 equals 10%; 8.5% profitability rate and 1.18 turnover rate also equals 10% ROI, and etc. Therefore, knowing one component will lead to decisions to generate the desired rate of the other component at a given rate of return.

Illustration of the Relationship of the
Profitability Rate and the Turnover Rate
at Different Levels of Return-on-Investment

5%		10%	
Profitability Rate X	Turnover Rate	Profitability Rate X	Turnover Rate
1.0%	5.00	1.0%	10.00
1.5	3.34	1.5	6.67
2.0	2.50	2.0	5.00
2.5	2.00	2.5	4.00
3.0	1.67	3.0	3.34
3.5	1.43	3.5	2.86
4.0	1.25	4.0	2.50
4.5	1.12	4.5	2.23
5.0	1.00	5.0	2.00
		5.5	1.82
		6.0	1.67
		6.5	1.54
		7.0	1.43
		7.5	1.34
		8.0	1.26
		8.5	1.18
		9.0	1.12
		9.5	1.06
		10.0	1.00

Detailing ROI Components

One of the interesting aspects of return-on-investment components, is that it can be broken down in a chart detailing all of the data affecting each components' calculation. By this breakdown, it is possible to see the behavioral pattern of each component, and the reasons for the effect on the overall return-on-investment rate. First, let's illustrate the profitability rate using the financial data previously presented in the Earnings Statement.

Profitability Rate

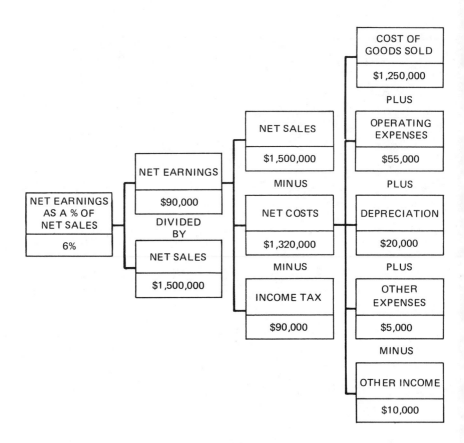

Note that each major income and expense item is charted which results into a profitability rate of 6%.

The turnover rate is also computed in a similar way and total assets will be used for the investment.

Turnover Rate

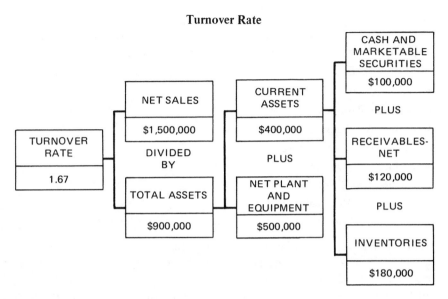

Each asset item is included and totals $900,000 of total assets. This divided by the net sales equals a turnover rate of 1.67 times.

The combination of both components results in a Return on Asset rate of 10%. This is computed as follows:

Return on Total Assets

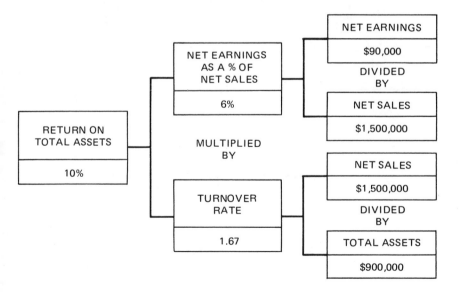

The profitability rate is multiplied by the turnover rate resulting in a 10% Return on Total Asset rate. Let's assume a company's next year's objective is 16%. In order to attain this rate, either the profitability rate and/or the turnover rate must change. Many decisions can be made as follows:

- Increase sales volume.
- Increase sales price.
- Reduce production costs.
- Reduce operating expenses.
- Reduce cash balances.
- Reduce receivables.
- Reduce inventory balances.
- Dispose of unprofitable facilities.

These are but some of the operating decisions that can be made to increase ROI rates. The type and magnitude of the changes will depend upon the achievable results that are desired. Some decisions may be easier than others. Remember, as pointed out earlier, decisions relating to the profitability rate may be easier to accomplish. This does not mean that areas relating to the turnover rate can not be accomplished. It does mean that greater earnings may be easier to accomplish due to greater control on expenses, particularly manpower costs.

    In summary, this same technique can be used to measure two different sets of data, that is, actual vs. budget, this year vs. last year, competitive companies, etc. This presents an excellent tool for analytical decisions, since it provides the individual items making up the two components, the profitability rate and the turnover rate.

CHAPTER 4

MEASURING MARKETING SEGMENTS USING ROI OBJECTIVES

Too often, sales territories are measured on sales performance only, and no recognition given to the amount of investment it may tie-up in the company. It is, therefore, possible to assign an investment base to a sales segment of the company and establish a true accountability center in the measurement of performance. The concept to be used will be referred to as Return on Controllable Assets. It will illustrate how evaluating marketing segments relates to the overall company objectives.

Return on Controllable Assets

This term is not mysterious, but implies that performance measurement will relate to the marketing side of the business. To further illustrate this concept, the two major components of ROI previously discussed will be used, namely, the profitability rate and the turnover rate. However, some changes in the elements will have to be made to accommodate evaluating only the marketing segment of the business.

The term Return on Controllable Assets consists of the following two components.

$$\frac{\text{Marketing Contribution}}{\text{Net Sales}} \times \frac{\text{Net Sales}}{\text{Controllable Assets}}$$

Marketing Contribution

Marketing contribution results from taking net sales by marketing territory, less cost of goods sold of those products anticipated to be sold, less selling expenses used by the marketing territory to sell the product. In the following illustration, total selling expenses will be used by sales region which represents the following expenses.

Salesmen's Salaries and Employee Benefits
Salesmen's Commissions
Manager's Override
Salesmen's Travel and Entertainment

Branch Expenses
Advertising
Telephone and Telegraph
Rent
Insurance and Taxes
Utilities
Repairs and Maintenance
Office Supplies
Postage
Depreciation
Miscellaneous

Net Sales By Marketing Territory

The total company's net sales are generated by four territories, namely, North, West, East and South. The total net sales relates to the previous Earnings Statement which indicates a total sales revenue of $1,500,000.

Controllable Assets By Sales Territory

Receivables and inventories are two assets that are controllable by the sales territory. Since net sales are generated by the sales territory, receivables are a function of net sales by sales territory. Net sales are generated by selling inventories and can be isolated by product line and sales territory. Therefore, for the purpose of this illustration, both receivables and inventories will be considered controllable assets. If other assets exist which are directly controllable by the sales territory, such as a company owned branch office, this would also be included in the controllable asset calculation.

The following schedule is presented by marketing territory and is based on a previous Earnings Statement and Balance Sheet.

Profitability By Marketing Territory

	North	West	East	South	Total
		Original			
Net Sales	$400,000	$300,000	$600,000	$200,000	$1,500,000
Cost of Goods Sold	320,000	255,000	500,000	175,000	1,250,000
Gross Profit	80,000	45,000	100,000	25,000	250,000
% to sales	20.0%	15.0%	16.7%	12.5%	16.7%
Selling	6,000	7,500	12,000	4,500	30,000
% to sales	1.5%	2.5%	2.0%	2.3%	2.0%
Marketing Contribution	$ 74,000	$ 37,500	$ 88,000	$ 20,500	220,000
% to sales	18.5%	12.5%	14.7%	10.3%	14.7%
Other Expenses					
General Expenses					15,000
Administrative Expenses					10,000
Depreciation					20,000
Other Income					(10,000)
Other Expense					5,000
Net Before Taxes					180,000
Income Taxes					90,000
Net Earnings					$ 90,000
Profitability Rate					6.0%
Controllable Assets					
Receivables	$ 40,000	$ 30,000	$ 35,000	$ 15,000	$ 120,000
Inventories	50,000	40,000	45,000	45,000	180,000
Total	$ 90,000	$ 70,000	$ 80,000	$ 60,000	$ 300,000
Turnover Rate	4.444	4.286	7.500	3.333	5.000
Other Assets					600,000
Total Assets					$ 900,000
Turnover Rate					1.667
Return on Controllable Assets	82.2%	53.6%	110.0%	34.2%	73.3%
Return on Total Assets					10.0%

Calculation

You will note that all of the data that effects a territory's return-on-investment is included, such as net sales from sales volume and sales mix; marketing contribution resulting from net sales less territory expenses and cost of goods sold; and controllable assets for each territory. As you will recall in previous calculations, the Return on Total Asset calculation was computed as follows:

$$\frac{\text{Net Sales}}{\text{Total Assets}} \quad \times \quad \frac{\text{Net Earnings}}{\text{Net Sales}} \quad = \quad \text{Return on Total Assets}$$

$$\frac{\$1,500,000}{\$\ \ 900,000} \quad \times \quad \frac{\$\ \ \ 90,000}{\$1,500,000} \quad = \quad 10\%$$

or

$$1.67 \text{ times} \quad \times \quad 6\% \quad = \quad 10\%$$

This can be broken down as follows:

	Marketing Contribution %	X	Marketing Turnover Rate	=	Return on Controllable Assets
North	18.5%		4.444		82.2%
West	12.5%		4.286		53.6%
East	14.7%		7.500		110.0%
South	10.3%		3.333		34.2%
Total Marketing Territories	14.7%		5.000		73.3%
Return on Total Assets					10.0%

You will note that each territory contributes a higher rate of return than the overall company. This is due to assets that do not directly contribute any sales dollars, but are necessary for the survival of the business, such as capital assets, cash, etc. However, in order to compensate for this, either higher objectives must be established for the sales territories, or reduce other areas of the company to a more productive basis. Assuming this has already been done, let's illustrate how the overall return on total assets can be increased by establishing certain revised objectives for the sales territories.

Assumptions

- Increase net sales by price increases on selected products, and changing sales mix to sell more higher priced products.
- Reduce selling expenses by instituting a more effective cost control program.
- Reduce receivables by tighter screening of customers and offering discounts for cash payments.
- Reducing inventories by disposing of obsolete and slow moving products.

Applying the assumptions to the original territorial data, the following schedule is presented.

Profitability By Marketing Territory

	North	Revised West	East	South	Total
Net Sales	$430,000	$315,000	$640,000	$215,000	$1,600,000
Cost of Goods Sold	344,000	267,750	533,120	188,125	1,332,995
Gross Profit	86,000	47,250	106,880	26,875	267,005
% to sales	20.0%	15.0%	16.7%	12.5%	16.7%
Selling	5,590	6,930	11,520	4,300	28,340
% to sales	1.3%	2.2%	1.8%	2.0%	1.8%
Marketing Contribution	$ 80,410	$ 40,320	$ 95,360	$ 22,575	238,665
% to sales	18.7%	12.8%	14.9%	10.5%	14.9%

Other Expenses

General Expenses	15,000
Administrative Expenses	10,000
Depreciation	20,000
Other Income	(10,000)
Other Expense	5,000
Net Before Taxes	198,665
Income Taxes	99,332
Net Earnings	$ 99,333
Profitability Rate	6.2%

Controllable Assets

	North	West	East	South	Total
Receivables	$ 36,000	$ 27,000	$ 33,000	$ 14,000	$ 110,000
Inventories	44,000	38,000	42,000	36,000	160,000
Total	$ 80,000	$ 65,000	$ 75,000	$ 50,000	$ 270,000
Turnover Rate	5.375	4.846	8.533	4.300	5.926

Other Assets					600,000
Total Assets					870,000
Turnover Rate					1.839
Return on Controllable Assets	100.5%	62.0%	127.1%	45.2%	88.4%
Return on Total Assets					11.4%

You will note that applying the revised assumptions increases the Return on Controllable Assets from 73.3% to 88.4% and the Return on Total Assets from 10.0% to 11.4%. The following comparisons are made between the original objectives versus the revised objectives.

	Original Objective	Revised Objective	Change
Return on Controllable Assets			
North	82.2%	100.5%	+18.3%
West	53.6	62.0	+ 8.4
East	110.0	127.1	+17.1
South	34.2	45.2	+11.0
Total	73.3%	88.4%	+15.1%
Return on Total Assets	10.0%	11.4%	+ 1.4%

The above indicates the impact of setting higher objectives in the sales territories on the overall corporate objective.

Sometimes it is not feasible to change all the factors at the same time which results in higher rates of return. The previous example reflects all assumption changes which resulted in a 1.4% increase in Return on Total Assets. It would be interesting to look at the results of Return on Total Assets by changing one factor at a time or several factors at the same time. The original assumptions resulted in the following:

Net Sales	$1,500,000
Marketing Contribution	220,000
% to sales	14.7%
Other Expenses – Net	40,000
Taxes	90,000
Net Earnings	$90,000
Profitability Rate	6%

Receivables — Net	$120,000
Inventories	180,000
Controllable Assets	$300,000
Turnover Rate	5.0
Other Assets	$600,000
Total Assets	$900,000
Turnover Rate	1.667
Return on Total Assets	10.0%

Net Sales

Increasing net sales ($100,000) and maintaining the same profitability rate (6.0%), the following results:

Profitability Rate	X	Turnover Rate	=	Return on Total Assets
$\dfrac{\$\ 96,000}{\$1,600,000}$	X	$\dfrac{\$1,600,000}{\$\ 900,000}$	=	10.7%
	or			
6%	X	1.778	=	10.7%

An increase in Return on Total Assets of .7% resulted due to a higher turnover rate of .111 times on higher net sales.

Marketing Contribution

The affect of increasing marketing contribution is as follows:

Profitability Rate	X	Turnover Rate	=	Return on Total Assets
$\dfrac{\$\ 99,333}{\$1,500,000}$	X	$\dfrac{\$1,500,000}{\$\ 900,000}$	=	11.0%
	or			
6.6%	X	1.667	=	11.0%

Controllable Assets

Lower controllable assets results in an increase of .3% on Return on Total Assets due to a higher turnover rate of .057 times.

Profitability Rate	X	Turnover Rate	=	Return on Total Assets
$\dfrac{\$\ \ 90,000}{\$1,500,000}$	X	$\dfrac{\$1,500,000}{\$\ \ 870,000}$	=	10.3%
	or			
6%	X	1.724	=	10.3%

This is just a few of the various ways by which sales management can reflect changes in Return on Total Assets. Changes in sales volume, sales mix and asset utilization must be fully evaluated by management in order to insure the highest maximization of Return on Assets to the company. As just illustrated, the Return on Asset rate can vary from 10.0% to 11.0% by influencing certain decisions relating to the marketing organization.

CHAPTER 5

COST OF CAPITAL

Cost of capital is that average rate of earnings which investors require to induce them to provide all forms of long-term capital to the company. Two major areas that generally involve the cost of capital and elements of capital are: internal decisions within a company as to how capital should be employed, i.e., which projects should be selected for investments; and deciding what outside sources should be used to provide the services, facilities, and funds needed to operate the business.

A company has many sources and variations of capital to choose from, such as equity and bank financing. Measuring the cost of capital can be calculated using several techniques. For example, one technique is opportunity cost, which measures the maximum yield from a specific investment that might have been earned if the investment had been applied to some alternative risk. Using the internal rate of return offers another approach, whereby measuring the discount rate which equates current or future cash flows with the original investment. The incremental cost technique states that any rate earned above the cost of financing is a favorable investment. For example, a capital investment earning 20% after borrowing from outside sources at 10% is a favorable investment. This is further supported by reviewing economic theory and a pronouncement made by Lord Keynes when he said, "businessmen would continue to invest as long as the return of one more dollar of investment (marginal efficiency of capital) exceeded the interest rate (marginal cost of capital)." From this statement, it appears that the incremental cost method makes sense and has substantial validity. Another technique is the weighted average cost approach. It is this method that calculations will be directed and reviewed.

Weighted Average Cost Method

Management has a responsibility in investing equity to insure that the minimum rate of return on the investment equals the return required to keep unchanged the value of the existing common equity. The cost of equity can be shown in two ways:

$$\text{Cost of Equity} \ = \ \frac{\text{Anticipated Earnings}}{\text{Net Price Per Share}}$$

or

$$\text{Cost of Equity} \ = \ \frac{\text{Dividends Per Share}}{\text{Net Price Per Share}} \ + \ \begin{array}{l}\text{Expected uniform annual} \\ \text{rate of growth of dividends}\end{array}$$

Assuming the following facts, each method is calculated:

Anticipated Earnings Per Share — $2.00
Net Price Per Share   — $20.00
Dividends Per Share   — $1.00
Growth Rate   —   5%

$$\frac{\$ \ 2.00}{\$20.00} = 10\% \ \text{ and } \ \frac{\$ \ 1.00}{\$20.00} + 5\% = 10\%$$

Under both methods, management must invest retained earnings in a capital investment that will earn at least 10% or market value of the share.

When a company uses more than one type of debt financing, it is necessary to develop a composite rate which is commonly referred to as the weighted average cost method. The calculated rate is the weighted average of the rates for long-term debt, preferred stockholders' equity, and common stockholders' equity. The following components of capital are presented:

Components of Capital			
Source	**Amount**	**Rate**	**Multiplication**
Long-Term Debt	$250,000	A	$250,000 A
Preferred Stockholders' Equity	100,000	B	100,000 B
Common Stockholders' Equity:			
Capital Stock	150,000		
Paid-in Surplus	50,000		
Retained Earnings	150,000		
Total	$350,000	C	$350,000 C
Total Capital	$700,000		D

The weighted average cost of capital is computed as follows:

$$\frac{D}{\$700,000}$$

A particular type of capital should not be associated with a particular investment proposal. One component of capital affects the cost of another. Capital should be viewed as a pool which results in an average cost from which funds are drawn for different capital investments.

Let's assume that the cost rate of long-term debt is 5.1%, which represents the yield rate on the net proceeds to the company on an after-tax basis. For example, a bond with a $100 face value is estimated to generate $98.00 net proceeds to a company after discounting and financing costs. In addition, the nominal interest is $10.00, or $5.00 after tax, resulting in 5.1% after tax cost rate ($5.00/$98.00).

Source	Amount	Rate	Multiplication
Long-Term Debt	$250,000	5.1%	$12,755

Assuming a similar example as above, the preferred stockholders' equity is as follows:

$$\frac{\$\ 8.00}{\$98.00} = 8.2\%$$

Source	Amount	Rate	Multiplication
Preferred Stockholders' Equity	$100,000	8.2%	$8,163

Of all the components, common stockholders' equity is the more difficult to handle in both concept and application. It must be determined whose cost is being measured; does in fact retained earnings have a cost; how is the cost measured; and what earnings per share should be used?

The cost to be measured is the stockholders' cost. From a stockholders' viewpoint, retained earnings has a cost. If retained earnings are retained in the business, the stockholders' cannot use it elsewhere to earn money, and also, has an opportunity cost. In theory, retention is the same as if the amount had been paid in dividends which were used to buy the company's stock. It is part of the money which the stockholder has invested in the ownership of the business. Therefore, it should be combined with the other common stock accounts in developing this cost measure.

The stockholders are investing because they expect to receive some benefits which will be almost equivalent to what they would receive on the next best investment when risk is considered. In addition, the stockholders are looking forward to two benefits which induce them to pay a price for the common stock. Dividends as they will be paid in the future and capital appreciation. Both benefits come from future earnings per share. It is the principal factor affecting the price of a stock in the long-run. The cost of capital is then measured by the inverse of the price-earnings ratio or the earnings-price ratio.

In computing the cost of common stockholders' equity, the net amount a company would receive from the sale of stock is divided into the future earnings per share as estimated by the investors. For example, the market price of the stock is $100, with financing costs of $15, results in net proceeds to the company of $85. This is divided into the future earnings per share estimated by the investors of $12, and results in a cost rate of 14.1%.

Source	Amount	Rate	Multiplication
Common Stockholders' Equity	$350,000	14.1%	$49,412

A summary of all three components is as follows:

Source	Amount	Rate	Multiplication
Long-Term Debt	$250,000	5.1%	$12,755
Preferred Stockholders' Equity	100,000	8.2%	8,163
Common Stockholders' Equity	350,000	14.1%	49,412
Total Capital	$700,000		$70,330

$$\text{Weighted Average Cost of Capital} = \frac{\$\,70,330}{\$700,000} = 10.0\%$$

The above weighted average cost of capital of 10.0% serves as the cut-off rate below which the company should not accept an investment proposal. If there were not capital investment proposals above the 10.0% rate, stockholders' presumably would be better off if they invested their capital in other investments. This rate also serves as part of long-range profit goals and forms a minimum goal for management to exceed in maximizing earnings. These goals are but part of the framework of a comprehensive and systematic program of management objectives.

Failure to Meet Cost of Capital

The impact of a company failing to meet its cost of capital can have many effects regarding the health of the company, both in the near-term, as well as the long-term. The most obvious is the higher cost of capital which increases, since more external financing is required to provide the necessary capital requirements of the company. This higher financing cost can lead to slower reinvestments which has unfavorable implications for the shareholder, and ultimately, the marketability of the company's stock.

With slower reinvestment, a company's growth may be impaired by having to reduce dividends. This decreases the shareholder's expectations and both the risk and return become less competitive in the marketplace. This in turn can cause the market value and the stock price to decline which completes the cycle. At this point, we are back to higher financing, and in some cases, unavailability of capital funds.

CHAPTER 6

CAPITAL INVESTMENTS

One of the key elements of a company's growth are investments in assets. These assets are part of the capital planning process and generally requires a longer period of return than the day-to-day expenditures required in the operations of a business. Recognizing the entrustment by the stockholders in the management of a company to both safeguard assets and generate higher earnings through the assets of a company, it is important to allocate funds in a priority order. It is assumed that most companies are not in a position to expend money for all projects requested, therefore, a mechanism must be established to handle capital expenditure requests and also to establish the necessary policies and procedures for selecting of those capital projects for which capital resources are available. That process which determines the allocation of funds in order of priority is referred to as the capital budgeting process.

Investments in assets can involve many types, as well as functions of a company. For example, it may include investments for increasing or maintaining revenue, manufacturing facilities, general administration and morale or image factors. These investments may be for physical assets, such as land, buildings, and machinery and equipment. Investments in working capital requirements such as cash and marketable securities, accounts receivables, and inventories, such as materials and supplies, work-in-process and finished goods can also be included. Other investments such as research and development, and administrative facilities are also included in the investments of a company.

Before a decision can be made, it is important to decide on the options available. The options may be to replace, add, do nothing, or decide to go out of business. These decisions require a great deal of analysis which involves many complex variables. The go or no go decision will be determined by answers to such questions as the effect of the financial structure and performance outcome of the company; economic and political considerations affected by the investment; acceptability by both internal and external factors; feasibility as it relates to a company's short and long-term objectives; alternative opportunities available; and most important, the availability of funds. When one considers the complexities of these factors, it is not all surprised that a great amount of manpower is spent in the capital expenditure process.

The capital investment process basically evolves around four steps. They are the planning and search for new opportunities; the economic worth and standards established for evaluation and decision making; the actual expenditure mechanism for monitoring cash; and the audit and post-completion process. Our discussion on capital investments will deal primarily with step two, that is, the economic worth and standards established for evaluation and decision making. The examination of techniques will be explored to guide management in making the correct decision by evaluating, weighing and measuring alternatives. It is through this process, that future growth of a company will result and provide the stockholders with an adequate return on capital and the ability of a company to compete within the marketplace.

Types of Capital Investments

Although capital asset classifications vary from company to company in capital budgeting, generally the following categories are used in identifying the type of asset to be considered for acquisition. This provides categories in which investment proposals are submitted in accordance with a company's policy and procedure which defines the mechanism for the selecting and acceptance of capital investments. It might be pointed out that certain types of investments do not require a return on the investment justification, since they are investments essential or necessary to the existence of the business. Without it, the only alternative is to go out of business, in the case of a product line, plant, or entire business. Other capital projects require a justification of the return-on-investment in determining the best alternative such as replacement investments, strategic investments and projects adding or expanding the business. However, in all cases, data should be submitted as outlined in the capital budgeting process.

Product Growth and Expansion Investments

These are projects that relate to new facilities and new products, and expansion of existing plants and products. These types of investments have profit potential, but contain risk, and can be difficult to estimate and develop a true evaluation. Such investments might include entry into new or existing markets with new products, improvement of existing products, additional capacity of new products, or a technological change in the nature of the product.

Maintaining Current Operations

These are investments that are essential to help the company continue and maintain its present position in the marketplace. Without these investments, such as repairs, replacements, and maintenance, the business would suffer a loss of earnings, and therefore, must be evaluated as to not only return-on-investment, but preventing loss of earnings to a business. These investments should also follow the guidelines as established by the capital budgeting process.

Cost Reduction Investments

These are investments where cost savings can be justified and ultimately, greater profits to the company. Cost savings might be definitive cost reductions as well as cost savings through greater efficiency.

Strategic Investments

These investments may not be capable of being measured, since they are areas where quantitative data cannot be generated. For example, measuring the numeric results of intangible employee benefits such as improving employee morale, and areas leading to the safety of employees, cannot be measured, since no tangible profit improvement may not be easy to isolate or specifically identify. However, it is known that not spending money for these investments will decrease productivity, and ultimately, lower profits. Every effort should be made to properly balance these investments with other investments generating profits. The same general policies and procedures should be followed as other investment categories.

Capital investment decisions, if successfully invested, provides the basis for establishing the growth of a company. Since profitability is a key factor, it is important to provide the tools to the decision makers so that quantified results are simplified down to a few simple indicators. The above investment categories will aid in developing the administrative policies and procedures in the utilization of return-on-investment concepts which will be discussed in detail later in this text. It is expected that a well managed capital expenditures program will generate the performance measurement looked upon by most profit companies, namely, higher net earnings.

DEPRECIATION

Depreciation is a system of accounting which allocates the investment cost less salvage/scrap value over the estimated useful life of the asset, in a systematic or rational manner, in an effort of insuring investment recovery. These assets are part of capital expenditures which are necessary for the production or sale of goods or services. Assets that are depreciable are classified as property, plant, and equipment or commonly known as fixed assets.

Useful Life of an Asset

In order to determine the length over which the asset will be depreciated, it is important to determine the useful life of the asset. The estimated useful life may be computed from economic, physical, technological changes, obsolescence, utilization or even governmental actions. While these conditions can dictate the estimated useful life of the asset, most businesses use guideline lives as established by the Internal Revenue Service. The following illustrates some of the groupings and life categories as published by the Internal Revenue Service.

Description of Assets	Asset Guideline Period
Office furniture, fixtures, and equipment	10 years
Transportation — Automobiles, taxis	3 years
Land Improvements	20 years
Office Buildings	45 years
Agriculture — Machinery and equipment, including grain bins and fences	10 years
Mining	10 years
Wholesale and retail trade	10 years
Manufacture of chemicals and allied products	11 years
Manufacture of glass products	14 years
Printing, publishing and allied industries	11 years
Motor Transport — Freight	8 years
Radio and television broadcasting	6 years
Water Utilities	50 years

These are but a sampling of guidelines established by the IRS. You will note the varying years established for different industries as well as different assets.

Salvage/Scrap Values

Although an asset may reach its estimated useful life, the asset may have some value at the time of disposal or replacement. This can be determined at the time of disposal and must be used as a cash inflow or cash outflow in the cash flow calculations for the last year of the useful life. Internal Revenue Codes may limit the amount of salvage/scrap values which can be used for tax purposes, and may generate a tendency towards using any salvage/scrap values in the cash flow calculations.

Methods of Depreciation

Depreciation can be based on as a function of use or as a function of time. When using depreciation based on use, it is necessary to estimate a common base such as units or hours. An example of using hours per unit of output as a base is as follows:

Cost of Machine $10,000

Estimated Life — 10,000 hours (5 years X 250 days/year
X 8 hours/day)

Machine hours —	Year 1	3,000
	Year 2	2,000
	Year 3	2,000
	Year 4	1,500
	Year 5	1,500

$$\frac{\$10,000}{10,000} = \$1.00 \text{ depreciation per hour}$$

Based on the number of hours the machine was operated for each year, the depreciation would be as follows:

Year	Depreciation Per Hour	Yearly Hours	Depreciation	% Depreciated
1	$1.00	3,000	$ 3,000	30%
2	1.00	2,000	2,000	50
3	1.00	2,000	2,000	70
4	1.00	1,500	1,500	85
5	1.00	1,500	1,500	100
Total	—	10,000	$10,000	—

Since problems of homogeneity and defining useful lives exist, depreciation based on time would be more acceptable.

Depreciation Based on Time

Three commonly used methods are the straight-line method, sum-of-the-years'-digits method, and double-declining balance method. The latter two methods are referred to as accelerated methods.

Straight-Line Method

This method is the most widely used due to its simplicity and generally easy to understand nature. This method allocates an equal portion of the investment over each period of use for the estimated life of the asset. It is computed as follows:

$$\text{Depreciation} = \frac{\text{Investment Cost} - \text{Scrap/Salvage Value}}{\text{Estimated Useful Life in Years}}$$

For example, an asset of $10,000 with a useful life of 5 years and no salvage/scrap value is computed as follows:

Year	Depreciation	Net Asset Value	% Depreciated
	–	$10,000	–
1	$2,000	8,000	20%
2	2,000	6,000	40
3	2,000	4,000	60
4	2,000	$ 2,000	80
5	2,000	–	100%
Total	$10,000	–	–

You can see that this method is easy to calculate and easy to understand. The periodic charge would be $2,000 per year or 20% a year as a percentage of the investment cost. The disadvantages of this method are that it ignores the time value of money and does not depreciate the asset according to its use. In other words, the more wear and tear on an asset, the less value the asset will have at the end of its useful life. Under the straight-line method, even charges are recorded without regard to wear and tear.

The effect of depreciation upon the evaluation of capital projects depends upon the method of depreciation used. For example, accelerated depreciation methods will shorten the payback period and result in a higher return-on-investment rate.

Sum-of-the-years'-digits Method

This method is an accelerated method of depreciation and is based on the sum of the digits for the estimated life of the asset which is used as the denominator. The numerator is each years' digit for each year of the estimated life. For example, an asset of $10,000 with an estimated 5 year life is computed as follows:

1) Each year is labeled numerically starting with 1,2,3,4 and 5. If the estimated life was 10 years, continuation of the numbering would be 6,7,8,9 and 10.

2) Calculate the sum-of-the-years'-digits for each years estimated life.

$$S = 1 + 2 + 3 + 4 + 5 = 15$$

3) A fraction is calculated for each years life as follows:

$$1/15 + 2/15 + 3/15 + 4/15 + 5/15$$

4) Apply the fraction starting with the last year and continue in reverse order to the amount of the asset to be depreciated.

Year	Fraction	Amount of Asset	Depreciation	% Depreciated
1	5/15	$10,000	$ 3,333	33.3%
2	4/15	10,000	2,667	60.0
3	3/15	10,000	2,000	80.0
4	2/15	10,000	1,333	93.3
5	1/15	$10,000	667	100.0%
Total	—	—	$10,000	—

Double-declining balance Method

This is another accelerated depreciation method and results in a higher amount of depreciation in the earlier years. This method is computed by applying a fixed rate (twice the rate of straight-line depreciation) to the undepreciated balance at the end of each year. However, at any given year when the amount of depreciation under the straight-line method is higher then the depreciation under the double-declining balance method, a change can be made to depreciate the remaining balance on a straight-line basis.

Year	Value of Asset at Beginning of Year	Rate	Depre- ciation	Value of Asset at End of Year	% Depre- ciated
1	$10,000	40%	$ 4,000	$6,000	40%
2	6,000	40	2,400	3,600	64
3	3,600	12	1,200	2,400	76
4	2,400	12	1,200	1,200	88
5	$ 1,200	12%	1,200	–	100%
Total	–	–	$10,000	–	–

Comparison of Depreciation Methods

In comparing the four methods, you will note that the asset value ($10,000) is fully depreciated after the estimated life of the asset (5 years). However, different charges are expensed each year resulting in differing cash flows, and ultimately differing payback periods and return-on-investment rates. Many companies will sacrifice lower returns for quicker paybacks in times of tight cash positions. Therefore, projects that recovers investment quicker are preferred over longer payback projects even though return-on-investment rates may be favorable. Each business must evaluate its own position regarding evaluation techniques. However, it might be pointed out that once an evaluation technique is established, including a depreciation method, that method must be consistently used to adhere to the consistently rule previously discussed. If a change occurs, previous calculations must be made to reflect current techniques. This is also true among various operations of a company who submit capital proposals. Each proposal must use the same evaluation techniques (including similar depreciation methods) in order to fully evaluate what projects take preference over others. Failure to do this, will result in not recognizing favorable investments, and ultimately, lower profits in future years.

Comparison of Depreciation Charges

Year	Number of Hours	Straight-Line	Sum-of-the-years'-digits	Double-Declining Balance
1	$ 3,000	$ 2,000	$ 3,333	$ 4,000
2	2,000	2,000	2,667	2,400
3	2,000	2,000	2,000	1,200
4	1,500	2,000	1,333	1,200
5	1,500	2,000	667	1,200
Total	$10,000	$10,000	$10,000	$10,000

Comparison of % Depreciated

Year	Number of Hours	Straight-Line	Sum-of-the-years'-digits	Double-Declining Balance
1	30.0%	20.0%	33.3%	40.0%
2	50.0	40.0	60.0	64.0
3	70.0	60.0	80.0	76.0
4	85.0	80.0	93.3	88.0
5	100.0%	100.0%	100.0%	100.0%

Different depreciation methods result in varying cash flows. You will note the different depreciation charges for each year under different methods ranging from $4000 in Year 1 under double-declining balance to $667 in Year 5 under sum-of-the-years'-digits method. In addition, varying percentages of the investment is depreciated in each year depending upon the method. Double-declining balance has the greatest amount of depreciation (64%) through the second year, but the sum-of-the-years'-digits method, write-off's the greatest amount of depreciation in Year 3 through the end of the investments life (5 years).

As indicated previously, accelerated depreciation methods (sum-of-the-years'-digits and double-declining balance) will result in higher cash flows in the earlier years, and thus, quicker payback and increased return-on-investment. Since both of these techniques rely on cash flows for its calculations, the use of accelerated depreciation accomplishes this in the computation of cash flows. The following illustrates using different depreciation methods and its effect on cash flows as reflected from a cash flow statement.

Straight-Line Method	1	2	3	4	5	Total
Net Income	$1200	$1850	$2450	$2750	$3100	$11350
Depreciation	2000	2000	2000	2000	2000	10000
Cash Inflow	$3200	$3850	$4450	$4750	$5100	$21350
% of Total	15.0%	18.0%	20.8%	22.2%	24.0%	100.0%

Sum-of-the-years' digits Method	1	2	3	4	5	Total
Net Income	$ 534	$1516	$2450	$3084	$3766	$11350
Depreciation	3333	2667	2000	1333	667	10000
Cash Inflow	$3867	$4183	$4450	$4417	$4433	$21350
% of Total	18.1%	19.6%	20.8%	20.7%	20.8%	100.0%

Double-Declining Balance Method	1	2	3	4	5	Total
Net Income	$ 200	$1650	$2850	$3150	$3500	$11350
Depreciation	4000	2400	1200	1200	1200	10000
Cash Inflow	$4200	$4050	$4050	$4350	$4700	$21350
% of Total	19.7%	19.0%	19.0%	20.3%	22.0%	100.0%

Even though total cash inflows do not change, the individual years change depending upon the depreciation method.

CASH FLOW

For purposes of capital expenditure evaluations, cash flow is computed as earnings after taxes plus depreciation. These figures relate to the incremental changes resulting from that particular project evaluation. In other words, only data relating to that particular project is used in computing cash flows. The computed cash flows must be part of the particular project under evaluation as if it were the only financial data available. The project must stand the test by itself without any data from other projects or other parts of the company's financial statement. To illustrate cash flow, the following case illustration is presented.

Case Illustration

A diversified manufacturing company is anticipating purchasing a machine for $10,000, with an expected life of 5 years at the time of purchase and no estimated salvage value. This piece of machinery will be depreciated on a straight-line basis. The machine is being purchased to increase unit production of an existing product due to an increasing market. Estimated unit volume at a unit sales price of $20.00 and variable unit costs of $8.00 are as follows:

	Estimated Units
Year 1	400
Year 2	500
Year 3	600
Year 4	650
Year 5	700

Fixed costs relating to the addition of this capital expenditure are as follows:

	Fixed Costs
Year 1	$400
Year 2	300
Year 3	300
Year 4	300
Year 5	$200

The tax rate is 50%. In addition, capital is needed for buildups of inventories and receivables as follows:

Year	**Inventories**	**Receivables**
1	($500)	($400)
2	(250)	(100)
3	(150)	(100)
4	150	100
5	$250	$150

Note: ( ) Brackets represents outflows of cash. Data without brackets represents inflows of cash.

Based on the above facts, the following Cash Flow Statement is presented:

Cash Flow Statement

	0	1	2	3	4	5
				Year		
Unit Volume		400	500	600	650	700
Net Sales – $20/unit		$ 8000	$10000	$12000	$13000	$14000
Variable Costs – $8/unit		3200	4000	4800	5200	5600
Fixed Costs		400	300	300	300	200
Depreciation		2000	2000	2000	2000	2000
Pre-Tax Income		2400	3700	4900	5500	6200
Taxes – 50%		1200	1850	2450	2750	3100
Net Income		1200	1850	2450	2750	3100
Depreciation (5yr-S/L)		2000	2000	2000	2000	2000
Cash Inflow		3200	3850	4450	4750	5100
Capital Investment	$(10000)					
Change in Inventories		(500)	(250)	(150)	150	250
Change in Receivables		(400)	(100)	(100)	100	150
Cash Outflow	(10000)	(900)	(350)	(250)	250	400
Net Cash Flow	(10000)	2300	3500	4200	5000	5500
Cumulative Cash Flow	$(10000)	$(7700)	$ (4200)	–	$ 5000	$10500

Note that depreciation is added back to net income to determine cash inflow, since depreciation is considered a non-cash item. It already has been included as an expense in the cost data, but provides a source of cash by reducing the amount of income tax payments. The following illustrates this point using data from Year 1 including depreciation and excluding depreciation.

	Including Depreciation	Excluding Depreciation
Net Sales	$8,000	$8,000
Less: Cash paid for material, labor and overhead (variable and fixed)	(3,600)	(3,600)
Less: Non-cash provision for depreciation	(2,000)	–
Pre-tax Profit	2,400	4,400
Income tax – 50%	(1,200)	(2,200)
Net Income	1,200	2,200

Add Non-cash provision for		
depreciation	2,000	–
Net Cash Flow	$3,200	$2,200

Note that depreciation provided an additional $1000, which represents 50% of the $2000 charge for that period of depreciation. In conclusion, although depreciation is not a direct source of cash, it does provide cash by reducing cash payments made for income tax payments.

CHAPTER 7

PAYBACK

The payback method measures the amount of time of a project's life in months and years, it takes to recoup from cash flows, the project's original investment. It is a method that is widely used, but is primarily used with another evaluation technique. This is due to the fact that the payback method does not measure profitability, but rather, cash recoverability.

When one refers to the payback method, other names such as the payback period method, cash-recovery period method, payout and payoff have been used. These identifications are basically the same techniques under different names, but may contain slight variations.

This method is popular due to the simplicity of its calculations as available from data submitted for capital expenditure proposals. It is also an excellent indicator of cash recoverability when cash is a major factor and may bear on the selection of investment alternatives. However, this method does not measure cash flows after the recoverability or payback period, and therefore, cannot be considered a true rate of return. Since many projects are long-term in nature, the payback method may be biased against projects which are important to a company's future growth.

Payback tends to minimize risk by pointing out the length of recovery time it takes and may be beneficial in evaluating projects that are heavily effected by economic and technological changes. Particularly, since greater weight is given to earlier cash flows and less weight to future cash flows.

Since payback does not measure profitability, ranking of capital proposals and comparisons or standards for measuring against absolute dollars do not exist. Also, too much emphasis is placed on liquidity, and capital recovery may often be confused with profits.

However, payback can be an indicator of profitability. Projects that pay back sooner, typically will have higher earnings in the short-run. Keep in mind, that using payback for this reason, may sacrifice future growth and ultimately, the value of the company.

To illustrate the calculation of the payback method, cash flows will be used from previous calculations.

Net Cash Flows		
Year	Yearly Net Cash Flows	Cumulative Net Cash Flows
0	$(10,000)	$(10,000)
1	2,300	(7,700)
2	3,500	(4,200)
3	4,200	–
4	5,000	5,000
5	$ 5,500	$ 10,000

To determine the payback period, focus on the cumulative net cash flows and determine in which year the cumulative net cash flows equal zero, or in what year do net cash flows equal the initial investment of $10,000. In this example, the zero point is 3 years. Therefore, the payback period is 3 years. The payback method can be expressed by a simple formula as follows:

$$P = I/NCF$$

P is the payback period which equals the initial investment (I), divided by the average net cash flow (NCF) from operations. However, this formula can only be used when net cash flows from operations (NCF) are annually uniform and computed over the life of the project. In this illustration, annual net cash flows from operations are not uniform.

An alternative method of computing payback is to use average yearly cash flows. This method is less accurate and not recommended when using accelerated depreciation methods, since it ignores the favorable cash flows generated from accelerated depreciation. The following computation results:

Average Net Cash Flow

$$\frac{\text{Total Net Cash Flows From Operations}}{\text{Number of Years}} = \frac{\$20,500}{5} = \$4,100$$

Payback

$$\frac{\text{Initial Investment}}{\text{Average Net Cash Flow}} = \frac{\$10,000}{\$ 4,100} = 2.439 \text{ years}$$

In most cases, cumulative net cash flows will not equal zero in even years, i.e., 1 year, 2 years, 3 years, etc., but rather, in fractions of a year or months. Under this situation, interpolation is required. Assuming the following net cash flows, the calculation of payback is as follows:

Net Cash Flows		
Year	Yearly Net Cash Flows	Cumulative Net Cash Flows
0	$(10,000)	$(10,000)
1	1,300	(8,700)
2	2,600	(6,100)
3	3,300	(2,800)
4	5,600	2,800
5	$ 7,700	$ 10,500

In this illustration, the zero point, or payback period, is between three and four years, since at the end of the third year, there still remains a cash outflow of $2,800 and a cash inflow of $2,800 for the fourth year. Therefore, the payback period is between three and four years. Since the data indicates that after three full years, the project is still in an outflow position, some portion of the fourth year's cash flow must be used to recover the investment of $10,000. A simple calculation of dividing the remaining cumulative net cash flows after the third year of $2,800 by the net cash flows for the fourth year of $5,600 results in a fraction of a year of .50 or 6 months (12 X .50). Therefore, the payback period is 3.5 years.

Payback Reciprocal

Another variation of the use of the payback method is the payback reciprocal. It must be recognized, that this method is merely a rough estimate of return-on-investment where the project life is at least twice the payback period method. In addition, it assumes that net cash flows are generated evenly each year. The formula is as follows:

$$P = NCF/I$$

Using the data from the average cash flow payback method, the following results:

$$P = \frac{\$ 4,100}{\$10,000} = 41.0\%$$

This mathematical approach is merely a rough tool and should not be used when the following conditions exist, since the margin of error would probably be considerable.

● When net cash flows differ from period to period.

- If salvage/scrap value is estimated to be significant at the end of the projects life.
- If the estimated projects life is similar from the payback period.

BAIL-OUT PAYBACK

As discussed previously, payback measures the amount of time it takes to recoup an investment from cash flows generated from the projects operation. This assumes that estimates of cash flow will materialize as projected. However, when measuring anticipated results of competing projects, it is advisable to use the bail-out payback method in measuring the project with the least risk, or how to avoid losses. This method will indicate what projects are a safer investment if it had to be abandoned.

Assuming we use the same data for the payback method, the payback period is as follows:

Year	Investment	Yearly Cash Flow	Cumulative Cash Flow
0	($10,000)	($10,000)	($10,000)
1		2,300	(7,700)
2		3,500	(4,200)
3		4,200	—
4		5,000	5,000
5		5,500	$10,500
	($10,000)	$10,500	

$$\text{Payback} = \frac{\text{Investment}}{\text{Yearly Cash Flow}} = \frac{\$10,000}{\$2,300+3,500+4,200} = 3.0 \text{ years}$$

For comparison purposes, lets assume an additional investment of $15,000 is proposed with the following yearly cash flows:

Year	Investment	Yearly Cash Flow	Cumulative Cash Flow
0	($15,000)	($15,000)	($15,000)
1		2,000	(13,000)
2		4,000	(9,000)
3		5,000	(4,000)
4		8,000	4,000
5		8,000	$12,000
	($15,000)	$12,000	

Payback calculation

Year 1 cash flow	$2,000	1.00 years
Year 2 cash flow	4,000	1.00 years
Year 3 cash flow	5,000	1.00 years
Year 3 cash flow remaining	4,000 X 1	.50 years
Year 4 cash flow	8,000	
Total years payback		3.50 years

The payback is 3.50 years as compared to 3.0 years for the previous investment. In order to consider the bail-out, it is necessary to include the salvage/scrap value of each investment proposal. Assume the first investment has a salvage/scrap value of $5,000 in year 1 and declines at an $800 annual rate. The second investment's salvage/scrap value is estimated to be $6,000 at the end of year 1 and decline $1,000 annually. The results follows:

Investment 1

Year	Cumulative Cash Flows	+	Salvage/ Scrap Value	=	Cumulative Total
1	$ 2,300		$5,000		$ 7,300
2	5,800		4,200		10,000

Investment 2

1	$ 2,000		$6,000		$ 8,000
2	6,000		5,000		11,000
3	11,000		4,000		15,000

The bail-out payback is when the cumulative cash flows plus salvage/scrap value at the end of any given year equals the original investment. In this illustration, the bail-out is 2 years for investment 1 and 3 years for investment 2. Therefore, investment 1 is the better investment because the investment will be recovered 1 year earlier. Compared to the traditional payback method, the bail-out method is favored since it does measure risk.

Discounted Payback Method

As will be discussed later, the introduction of the interest factor relating to the cost of money, can be applied as a variation to the payback method, and is referred to as the discounted payback method. A discount factor is applied to the net cash flows and a payback period is calculated as follows:

Discounted Net Cash Flows			
Year	Yearly Net Cash Flows	Discount Factor @ 25%	Present Values
0	$(10,000)	1.000	$(10,000)
1	2,300	.800	1,840
2	3,500	.640	2,240
3	4,200	.512	2,150
4	5,000	.410	2,050
5	5,500	.328	1,804
	$ 10,500		$ 84

You can see that the payback period is slightly over 5 years and is longer than the original payback period of 3 years. It is calculated by applying a 25% discount rate, since it is this rate that the discounted net cash flows approximately equal zero. There is an additional $84 to be recovered which means that the actual discount rate is 25+%. Any higher discount rate would result in a longer than a 5 year payback. Further discussion will be given on discounted cash flows (DCF).

Decision Guidelines

Through another variation of the payback method, the ability to set decision guidelines which will eliminate those projects having lower than desired minimums can be established. In otherwords, only projects meeting the desired minimum objectives would be accepted. This theory uses the Present Value of $1.00 Received Annually for N Years Table. This table shows the present value of $1.00 received annually for each of the next n years if i annual rate of return is earned on the remaining balance of the original investment throughout the period. The following is a sample of such a table:

Years	Interest (i)			
(N)	8%	10%	12%	14%
1	0.926	0.909	0.893	0.877
2	1.783	1.736	1.690	1.647
3	2.577	2.487	2.402	2.322
4	3.312	3.170	3.037	2.914
5	3.993	3.791	3.605	3.433

For example, a project with a useful life of 5 years with an expected rate of return of 10%, should have a maximum payback of 3.791 years. The higher the interest rate and longer the projects useful life, the shorter the maximum payback will be. Conversely, the lower the interest rate and shorter the projects useful life, the higher the maximum payback will be.

However, only projects that have even net cash flows can use this method. When net cash flows are uneven, this method is not recommended.

CHAPTER 8

ACCOUNTING METHODS

The accounting method of measuring capital investments follows close to the conventional methods of generally accepted accounting principles in recording income and investments. It makes use of data as presented on financial statements familiar to most business people. Many variations of the accounting method can be used, depending on the numerator and the denominator selected. Each variation will result in different ratios, but as long as the same ratios are used for evaluating projects, i.e., the rule of consistency, proper evaluation will result in comparing investment decisions.

The term accounting method is also known as the book-value rate of return, the accounting rate of return, the approximate rate of return, and the unadjusted rate of return. Within the basic terminology, there are many different calculations. All relate to generally accepted financial statements and any method is acceptable, assuming the rule of consistency is applied.

Before illustrations are presented, it is important to briefly highlight the advantages and disadvantages of using accounting methods as a tool for evaluating capital investments.

Advantages

- Easy to calculate, since basically three components are needed: investment value, estimated life of a project, and estimated net earnings. Since this data is necessary to complete a capital investment proposal, the data is readily available and is easy to calculate and understand.
- This method emphasizes the profit and loss effect of a capital investment rather than the effect of cash flows.

- Relates to accounting data and therefore, presents a favorable means of measuring forecasted data with historical accounting records. Interpretation of capital investment performance is made easy, since it follows the same guidelines as used in a company's generally accepted accounting principles.

Disadvantages

- Does not recognize the time value of money. Discounted cash flow techniques will be discussed in later material.
- Assumes that a capital project will last for the depreciable life. When in reality, this is generally not true.
- Accounting data is not always consistent from year to year, that is, changes are made such as inventory evaluations, depreciation methods, capitalization vs. expense items, etc., which may lead to unfounded conclusions.
- Assumes equal weight is given to cash flows for all years.
- Assumes all projects are similar in nature to each other. Most capital investments vary, therefore, this method may be considered undesirable.
- Since this method follows generally accepted accounting principles, non-accounting personnel may be limited by not having extensive accounting knowledge.

Methods of Calculation

The following methods are a sampling of the variations that exist in the computation of the accounting method. This is due to the variations of net earnings and computation of investment. Keep in mind, that any variation is correct as long as it is consistently used for all project evaluations. The following assumptions are made for illustration purposes.

Original Investment — $100,000
No Salvage/Scrap Value
Estimated Depreciable Life — 5 years
Depreciation Method — Straight-Line
Yearly Net Earnings (After Taxes) — $30,000

Annual Return on Original Investment

$$\frac{\text{Annual Net Earnings}}{\text{Original Investment}} \times 100$$

$$\frac{\$\ 30{,}000}{\$100{,}000} \times 100 = 30.0\%$$

Annual Return on Average Investment

$$\frac{\text{Annual Net Earnings}}{\dfrac{\text{Original Investment}}{2}} \times 100$$

$$\frac{\$\ 30{,}000}{\dfrac{\$100{,}000}{2}} \times 100 = 60.0\%$$

Average Book Return on Investment

$$\frac{\text{Total Net Earnings} - \text{Original Investment}}{\text{Weighted Average Investment}^*} \times 100$$

$$\frac{\$150{,}00 - \$100{,}000}{\$300{,}000} \times 100 = 16.7\%$$

*Computation of Weighted Average Investment

Year	Original Investment	−	Accumulated S/L Deprec.	=	Book Values
0	$100,000		−		$100,000
1	100,000		$ 20,000		80,000
2	100,000		40,000		60,000
3	100,000		60,000		40,000
4	100,000		80,000		20,000
5	$100,000		$100,000		−
	Weighted Average Investment				$300,000

Average Return on Average Investment

$$\frac{\text{Total Net Earnings} - \text{Original Investment}}{\dfrac{\text{Original Investment}}{2} \times \text{Estimated Depreciable Life}} \times 100$$

$$\frac{\$150{,}000 - \$100{,}000}{\dfrac{\$100{,}000}{2} \times 5} \times 100 = 20.0\%$$

The following summarizes the different rates using the various calculations:

Method of Calculation	Rate
Annual Return on Average Investment	60.0%
Annual Return on Original Investment	30.0%
Average Return on Average Investment	20.0%
Average Book Return on Investment	16.7%

You can see that the selection of the method will vary the rate of return. Remembering the consistency rule and choosing one method, will properly assist in the evaluation of capital investments.

CHAPTER 9

DISCOUNTED CASH FLOW

The discounted cash flow method computes the rate of interest which equals the value of all future cash inflows attributable to the investment (cash outflow) at a given point in time. DCF calculations result in all cash inflows and outflows being equal. The theory is, "a dollar today is worth more than a dollar in the future." The general lack of understanding of this method is partly due to measuring the future time value of money.

A student of DCF will discover that terminologies vary when referring to discounted cash flow techniques. While the terms may vary, the basic concept of the time value of money is always present. Terms describing DCF are discounted cash flow, net present value, time adjusted rate of return, the investor's method, interest rate of return, present worth, profitability index, marginal efficiency of capital, and the scientific method. For illustration purposes, discounted cash flow (DCF) will be used to describe the basic concept. However, other terms will be used when referring to other variations of DCF. Keep in mind, that all terms used in this chapter refer to evaluating capital investments using the time value of money.

It is important for the understanding of the concept to briefly highlight the advantages and disadvantages using DCF methods.

Advantages

- Considers the time value of money.
- Common denominator for all types of projects, thereby allowing comparisons of different types of investments, including lease arrangements.
- Considers the cash flows from the life of the investment.

65

- Facilitates ranking of projects.
- Evaluates the components of the earnings statement as expenditures and revenues are recorded.

Disadvantages

- Assumes cash flows can be reinvested at the calculated discount rate.
- More difficult to calculate and understand.
- No relationship to accounting records or book profit and loss effects.
- Uncertainty of forecasted cash flows.

Understanding The Concept

To understand DCF, it is important to understand the time value of money. It must be recognized that a dollar today is worth more than a dollar to be received or spent in x years from now. The one common denominator that is used is the interest rate. To understand DCF, one must understand compounding.

Compounding

Assume you deposit $1,000 in a savings account at 8% annual interest, how much will you have after 5 years?

Year	Principal	Interest @ 8%	Total
0	$1,000	–	$1,000
1	1,000	$ 80	1,080
2	1,080	86	1,166
3	1,166	93	1,259
4	1,259	101	1,360
5	$1,360	109	$1,469

You can see that $1,000 deposited today, will be worth $1,469 in five years, or $469 interest earned. To simplify the calculation, a formula can be used whereby, a factor would be applied to the principal at a given rate for a given amount of time and arrive at the same amount as calculated above. The formula for computing compound interest is $P(1 + r)^n$ or to what amount will $1.00 grow, if it earns r interest compounded for n periods. The following is a sampling of a compound interest table for a limited amount of periods (n) and a limited amount of interest rates (r).

n	6%	8%	10%
0	1.0000	1.0000	1.0000
1	1.0600	1.0800	1.1000
2	1.1236	1.1664	1.2100
3	1.1910	1.2597	1.3310
4	1.2625	1.3605	1.4641
5	1.3382	1.4693	1.6105

Referring to the illustration, it was calculated that a $1,000 in a savings account at 8% interest for five years is worth $1,469 or an increase of 46.9%. This involved a series of calculations and can be simplified by applying the compound interest factor of 1.4693 to the $1,000 and arriving at $1,469. This is referred to as compounding.

Discounting

The interesting thing about compounding is that it is the reverse of discounting. For example, using the above mentioned compounding techniques, the value of money is shifted from the present into the future. The discounting concept shifts the value of money to be received in the future back to the present. In the compounding illustration, we determined that $1,000 invested today at 8% interest for five years is worth $1,469. Under discounting, we want to know if I need $1,000 in five years, how much must I deposit today, earning 8% annual interest?

Year	Principal	Interest − 8%	Total
0	$1,469	1.00000	$1,469
1	1,469	.92593	1,360
2	1,469	.85734	1,259
3	1,469	.79383	1,166
4	1,469	.73503	1,080
5	1,469	.68058	1,000

You can see that present values of $1,469 due at the end of 5 years is $1,000. The formula for computing the present value is $\frac{X}{(1 + r)^n}$. A sampling of present value tables for a limited number of periods (n) and a limited number of interest rates (r) are as follows:

n	6%	8%	10%
0	1.00000	1.00000	1.00000
1	.94340	.92593	.90909
2	.89000	.85734	.82645
3	.83962	.79383	.75131
4	.79209	.73503	.68301
5	.74726	.68058	.62092

To calculate the rate at which $1,469 will equal the original investment of $1,000 requires a trial and error. This will be discussed later in the text. However, assuming the rate is 8%, we can refer to the above table and multiply the discount factor of .68058 to the $1,469 and arrive back at the $1,000 original investment.

$$\$1,469 \ \text{X} \ .68058 = \$1,000$$

Therefore, if I need $1,000 in five years, I must deposit $1,469 today at 8% annual interest.

Reciprocal

The compound interest rates and the present value factors are reciprocal to each other. For example, a summary of both the compound interest factors and the present value factors are presented below.

Interest Rate at 8%

Number of Periods	Compound Factors	X	Present Value Factors	=	Reciprocal
0	1.0000		1.00000		1
1	1.0800		.92593		1
2	1.1664		.85734		1
3	1.2597		.79383		1
4	1.3605		.73503		1
5	1.4693		.68058		1

Since, when the compound factors are multiplied by the present value factors and the results equal one, it is concluded the reverse of compounding is discounting. Therefore, it is possible to find either the compound factor or the present value factor by knowing either of one factor.

Selecting A Discount Rate

In determining what discount rate to use, it is important to select a rate which coincides with a company's objective. This objective may be a company's cost of capital, corporate rate of return, corporate rate plus an additional percent, industry averages, governmental regulations, or any other combination. It is this rate to which capital investments should be at least the minimum rate to be acceptable. However, there may be projects which are necessary to the existence of the business and do not generate any returns to the company. These projects should be kept at a minimum. The minimum cut-off rate should be high enough to absorb these types of projects as well as costs which do not generate any profits to the company such as overhead. Caution should be noted that when selecting projects that have slight differences in the return rate, further analysis should be given, since present values are merely based on estimates. Margin of error can exist in estimating cash flows.

Calculation of DCF

The calculation of discounted net cash flow starts with the net cash flows as estimated from the capital investment proposal. These net cash flows are discounted through a trial and error, whereby the discounted net cash flows for the estimated life result in a zero balance. Using the illustration of the cash flow statement, the following schedule is presented. Keep in mind, that these net cash flows, when discounted, must equal the original investment of $10,000.

| | | Trial #1 | | Trial #2 | |
| | | Present Value at 24% | | Present Value at 26% | |
Year	Net Cash Flow	Factor	DCF	Factor	DCF
0	($10,000)	1.00000	($10,000)	1.00000	($10,000)
1	2,300	.80645	1,855	.79365	1,825
2	3,500	.65036	2,276	.62988	2,205
3	4,200	.52449	2,203	.49991	2,100
4	5,000	.42297	2,115	.39675	1,984
5	5,500	.34111	1,876	.31488	1,732
	P.V. $10,500		$ 325		($ 154)

The calculation indicates that the discount rate is between 24% and 26%. You can see that discounting at 24% leaves $325 of cash inflow and at 26%, ($154) to be recovered of the cash outflow. Through interpolation, the correct discount rate is 25.4%. This means that if the annual net cash flows were discounted at the 25.4% rate, the net discounted cash flows would equal zero. Interpolation is calculated as follows:

$$24\% + \left(2\% \times \frac{\$325}{\$479}\right) = 25.4\%$$

Effect of Accelerated Depreciation on DCF Rate

It was pointed out earlier, that net cash flows in the earlier years are more meaningful than future net cash flows. Therefore, using accelerated depreciation methods increases the discounted rate. The net cash flows in the previous illustration have been adjusted to reflect double-declining balance method of depreciation. The net cash flows are as follows:

Year	Net Cash Flows
1	$3,300
2	3,700
3	3,800
4	4,600
5	5,100

Using the same trial and error technique, the following results:

		Trial #1		Trial #2	
		Present Value at 26%		Present Value at 28%	
Year	Net Cash Flow	Factor	DCF	Factor	DCF
0	($10,000)	1.00000	($10,000)	1.00000	($10,000)
1	3,300	.79365	2,619	.78125	2,578
2	3,700	.62988	2,331	.61035	2,258
3	3,800	.49991	1,900	.47684	1,812
4	4,600	.39675	1,825	.37253	1,714
5	5,100	.31488	1,606	.29104	1,484
P.V.	$10,500		$ 281		($ 154)

The discount rate is somewhere between 26% and 28%. Interpolation results in a 27.29% discount rate.

$$26\% + \left(2\% \times \frac{\$281}{\$435}\right) = 27.29\%$$

This compares to the previous calculated discount rate of 25.4% under straight-line depreciation. In summary, accelerated depreciation methods increase the discount rate. Whichever method is chosen, this method should be consistently used in evaluating capital investment decisions.

NET PRESENT VALUE

Another variation of discounted cash flow is the net present value method. This technique is calculated by computing the net present values of the expected net cash flows, using the desired minimum rate of return as the discount rate. The total of the net present values are subtracted from the original capital investment, with the following investment decisions. If the net present values is positive or zero, the project should be accepted; if negative, the project should be rejected. If the projects under review are mutually exclusive, the project with the higher net present values would be selected.

The same concepts apply as discussed for DCF, that is, earlier net cash flows are preferred over projects generating net cash flows in later years.

Illustration

The following procedures are used in computing net present values:

1. Estimated future net cash flows are derived from the capital investment proposal.

2. Select a discount rate in keeping with the company's objective.

3. Refer to discount tables for discount factors under selected discount rate for estimated life of the investment.

4. Calculate the net present values by multiplying the net cash flows by the discount factors for each year.

5. Add all net present values for all years. If positive, the investment is anticipated to be profitable. If negative, it is anticipated that the investment will not generate a favorable profit or insufficient to recover the original investment. Using the data as presented for DCF, the following net present values are computed at a 24% discount rate.

Year	Net Cash Flows	Discount Factor @ 24%	Total Present Values
1	$ 2,300	.80645	$ 1,855
2	3,500	.65036	2,276
3	4,200	.52449	2,203
4	5,000	.42297	2,115
5	5,500	.34111	1,876
	$20,500		$10,325
		Less: Original Investment	10,000
		Net Present Value	$ 325

This investment is desirable since the company could invest $325 more, or a total of $10,325 and still earn 24% on the investment. Notice that the same conclusion was drawn from DCF calculations. However, in the net present value technique, net present values are looked upon as positive or negative, as compared to DCF calculations whereby, a rate is determined which equals or exceeds the minimum desired rate of return.

Excess Present Value Index (EPV)

A variation of the net present value technique is called the excess present value index (EPV). This method uses net present values and expresses the results in the form of an index. The primary use is to put investments of different types and levels on an equal basis for ranking purposes.

Referring to previous data, assume the company has an alternative of spending $10,000 for one project, or two investments of $5,000 each. Net present values for each of the two investments are $5,500. The following is presented:

	Proposed	Alternatives 1	2
Investment	$10,000	$5,000	$5,000
Net Present Values	10,325	5,500	5,500
Excess Present Value	$ 325	$ 500	$ 500
Excess Present Value Index	1.0325	1.1000	1.1000

The above illustration indicates that the EPV index for the original investment was 1.0325 indicating that this investment will return $1.0325 of investment from present values. You will note that the discounting rate was 24%, which is the same as the calculation for the net present value technique. Instead of interpreting the results as a total of present values, the results are interpreted as an index, or the ratio of total present values ($10,325), divided by the original investment of $10,000.

Interpreting the results would lead to the conclusion that the company would be advisable to spend $10,000 for the two separate projects of $5,000 each. The EPV index is 1.1000 for each of the alternatives versus 1.0325 for the one $10,000 investment. In addition, the sum of the excess present values are higher for the alternative investment ($1,000) as compared to $325 for the one investment. In summary, when faced with a group of alternative investments, it is advisable to use the EPV index as a screening technique when limited amounts of capital are available.

CHAPTER 10

LEASING

In previous chapters, discussion centered around the acquisition of capital investments and the evaluation techniques associated with the acquiring of capital assets. No reference was given to how the investment was to be acquired. There are three basic types of financing alternatives available. They are purchasing by cash, borrowing money from a bank, and some form of lease arrangement. This chapter will deal with the basic concept of leasing and the comparisons of leasing versus cash purchase and term financing.

Leasing is simply another way of using capital investments by renting as opposed to buying. A more classical definition of leasing is a contract whereby one party (lessor) conveys the use of a capital asset to another party (lessee) for a specified rate for a specified term of years. It is assumed that a company can utilize its capital and credit line to greater advantage since leasing does not require heavy outlays of capital in the initial years. However, it must be recognized that if total lease payments were compared to the total purchase price, leasing would appear to be more costly.

Leasing assumes "pay-as-you-use" without actually owning the asset. During inflationary periods, this can be advantageous by providing payment with cheaper dollars in future years. However, it is important to point out that leasing may not be advantageous for some companies. Financial conditions of the company in terms of capital structure, income tax provisions, and use of cash flow may prohibit or discourage leasing. An opinion of your tax counsel is advised before entering into any lease arrangement.

Lease Evaluations

Many techniques can be used for evaluating lease proposals. These techniques are also used in evaluating cash flows for capital expenditures. Before any technique is used, it is important to establish whether or not the acquisition of an asset is desirable. To arrive at a conclusion, it is necessary to measure the expected profitability of a capital investment and compare the results with the company's minimum acceptable return-on-investment. Previously, the methods of capital investment evaluation as well as setting company objectives were discussed. It is important at this time to distinguish between two types of measurement. The first type of return-on-investment is the return expected from funds expended for capital investments, and measures the profitability of a proposed capital investment through the use of funds, and comparing that with the cost rate derived from the source of funds. The other type of measurement is the return investors expect for the use of their funds. Since the cost of capital is that rate which is required to attract investment, it can be used as the base for establishing an overall minimum rate of return for capital investment proposals.

Lease versus Cash Purchase

When comparing leasing vs. a cash purchase, leasing provides many advantages:

- Way of conserving capital.
- Provides favorable cash flows in earlier years.
- Can offer tax advantages.
- Considered an effective hedge against inflation.
- In some companies, leasing avoids rigid capital expenditure procedures.
- Aids in forecasting cash requirements.
- Method of trying machinery and equipment before committing to purchase.
- In many cases, acquiring asset is easier.
- Provides the means to obtain machinery and equipment to meet seasonal production.

The following basic assumptions are presented for illustration purposes. Keep in mind, that different assumptions may lead to different conclusions. For example, such items as investment tax credit limitations, tax rates, depreciation methods, salvage/scrap value, cash position, and ability to borrow capital, may conclude the purchasing of an asset for cash as opposed to leasing, or vice-versa. Each comparison must be proven to be financially sound and must also meet the objectives of the company.

Assumptions

Cost of Asset — $100,000   Investment Tax Credit — 10%
Depreciable Life — 10 years   Tax Rate — 50%
Depreciation Method —   Lease Term — 10 years
  Sum-of-the-years'-digits   Monthly Rental Payments —
Salvage/Scrap Value — 0   120 payments of $1100

Based on the above assumptions, the following net cash costs are computed for a lease and a cash purchase.

	Lease		
Year	Lease Payment	Tax Effect	Net Cash Cost
0	–	–	–
1	$ 13,200	$(6,600)	$ 6,600
2	13,200	(6,600)	6,600
3	13,200	(6,600)	6,600
4	13,200	(6,600)	6,600
5	13,200	(6,600)	6,600
6	13,200	(6,600)	6,600
7	13,200	(6,600)	6,600
8	13,200	(6,600)	6,600
9	13,200	(6,600)	6,600
10	13,200	(6,600)	6,600
	$132,000	$(66,000)	$66,000

		Cash Purchase			
Year	Cost	Investment Tax Credit	Sum-of-the-years' digits	Tax Effect of Depreciation	Net Cash Cost
0	$100,000	–	–	–	$100,000
1		$(10,000)	$ 18,182	$(9,091)	(19,091)
2			16,364	(8,182)	(8,182)
3			14,545	(7,273)	(7,272)
4			12,727	(6,364)	(6,363)
5			10,909	(5,455)	(5,454)
6			9,091	(4,545)	(4,546)
7			7,273	(3,636)	(3,637)
8			5,455	(2,727)	(2,728)
9			3,636	(1,818)	(1,818)
10			1,818	(909)	(909)
	$100,000	$(10,000)	$100,000	$(50,000)	$ 40,000

The following is a comparison of cumulative net cash costs and the additional available cash through leasing vs. cash purchase.

	Cumulative Net Cash Costs		
Year	Lease	Cash Purchase	Available Cash Through Leasing
0	–	$100,000	$100,000
1	$ 6,600	80,909	74,309
2	13,200	72,727	59,527
3	19,800	65,455	45,655
4	26,400	59,092	32,692
5	33,000	53,638	20,638
6	39,600	49,092	9,492
7	46,200	45,455	(745)
8	52,800	42,727	(10,073)
9	59,400	40,909	(18,491)
10	$66,000	$ 40,000	$ (26,000)

This illustration highlights the fact that leasing conserves cash during the equipment's productive years. During the first six years, the cash available through leasing is favorable by $9,492. However, for the remaining four years, a cash purchase is favorable. You can see that over the life of the lease, additional cash is needed ($26,000), however, expenditures of capital have been delayed and assumed that this capital is productively put to use.

To fully analyze the cash advantages or disadvantages of leasing versus cash purchasing, a comparison of both methods is necessary. Applying discounted cash flow techniques, the net cash costs are computed for both leasing and a cash purchase, and a present value factor applied to each year's net cash cost. The selection of a discount rate, assumes that the capital conserved by the use of leasing can be reinvested into other investment opportunities yielding at least the discount rate, which in this case is 10%.

Lease			
Year	Net Cash Costs	Present Value Factor @ 10%	Present Values
0	–	1.00000	–
1	$ 6,600	.90909	$ 6,000
2	6,600	.82645	5,455
3	6,600	.75131	4,959
4	6,600	.68301	4,508
5	6,600	.62092	4,098
6	6,600	.56447	3,726
7	6,600	.51316	3,387
8	6,600	.46651	3,079
9	6,600	.42410	2,799
10	6,600	.38554	2,546
	$66,000		$40,557

Cash Purchase			
Year	Net Cash Costs	Present Value Factor @ 10%	Present Values
0	$100,000	1.00000	$100,000
1	(19,091)	.90909	(17,355)
2	(8,182)	.82645	(6,762)
3	(7,272)	.75131	(5,464)
4	(6,363)	.68301	(4,346)
5	(5,454)	.62092	(3,386)
6	(4,546)	.56447	(2,566)
7	(3,637)	.51316	(1,866)
8	(2,728)	.46651	(1,273)
9	(1,818)	.42410	(771)
10	(909)	.38554	(350)
	$ 40,000		$ 55,861

The following is a cumulative comparison of net cash costs after present value factors have been applied.

Cumulative Present Value Net Cash Costs			
Year	Lease	Cash Purchase	Available Cash Through Leasing
0	–	$100,000	$100,000
1	$ 6,000	82,645	76,645
2	11,455	75,883	64,428
3	16,414	70,419	54,005
4	20,922	66,073	45,151
5	25,020	62,687	37,667
6	28,746	60,121	31,375
7	32,133	58,255	26,122
8	35,212	56,982	21,770
9	38,011	56,211	18,200
10	$40,557	$ 55,861	$ 15,304

Under discounted cash flow techniques, leasing provides favorable capital throughout the life of the asset, but as mentioned, it is assumed that the available capital generated through leasing, can be reinvested in profitable investments at a 10% rate after taxes.

Lease versus Term Financing

Leasing can be viewed as an alternate source of financing. It generally conserves existing bank credit lines for other investment purposes such as working capital requirements, and allows the full use of a company's borrowing capacity. Unlike financing, leasing may not require public disclosure of financial data. However, under certain conditions, lease arrangements may be required such as in a prospectus for a public offering. When financing through the sale of securities, dilution of ownership occurs, which is avoided through a lease arrangement. Other advantages such as 100% financing, flexible and long term agreements, and easier documentation, favor leasing over term financing. As in the case of leasing vs. cash purchase, each lease arrangement must be treated individually for benefits to be derived, and should be reviewed with a company's tax counsel. Referring to the previous illustration of a lease arrangement vs. cash purchase, let's assume a comparison between a lease arrangement and term financing. The lease data is unchanged, but is compared to a term loan of five years, plus 10% interest rate, and a payment schedule of 60 monthly payments of $1,666.66 plus interest. The following reflects the net cash costs assuming the above data.

Term Financing				
Year	Total Payments	Investment Tax Credit	Tax Effect of Depreciation	Tax Effect of Interest	Net Cash Cost
1	$ 29,083	$(10,000)	$(9,091)	$(4,542)	$ 5,450
2	27,417		(8,182)	(3,708)	15,527
3	25,750		(7,273)	(2,875)	15,602
4	24,083		(6,364)	(2,042)	15,677
5	22,417		(5,455)	(1,208)	15,754
6			(4,545)		(4,545)
7			(3,636)		(3,636)
8			(2,727)		(2,727)
9			(1,818)		(1,818)
10			(909)		(909)
	$128,750	$(10,000)	$(50,000)	$(14,375)	$54,375

Applying a 10% present value factor results in the following:

Term Financing			
Year	Net Cash Costs	Present Value Factor @ 10%	Present Values
0	–	1.00000	–
1	$ 5,450	.90909	$ 4,955
2	15,527	.82645	12,832
3	15,602	.75131	11,722
4	15,677	.68301	10,708
5	15,754	.62092	9,782
6	(4,545)	.56447	(2,566)
7	(3,636)	.51316	(1,866)
8	(2,727)	.46651	(1,272)
9	(1,818)	.42410	(771)
10	(909)	.38554	(350)
	$54,375		$43,174

A comparison is made of cumulative present value net cash costs of leasing vs. term financing.

Cumulative Present Value Net Cash Costs			
Year	Lease	Term Financing	Available Cash Through Leasing
1	$ 6,000	$ 4,955	$(1,045)
2	11,455	17,787	6,332
3	16,414	29,509	13,095
4	20,922	40,217	19,295
5	25,020	49,999	24,979
6	28,746	47,433	18,687
7	32,133	45,567	13,434
8	35,212	44,295	9,083
9	38,011	43,524	5,513
10	$40,557	$43,174	$ 2,617

With the exception of the first year, leasing is advantageous over term financing during the life of the lease. In summary, leasing presents a favorable form of capital asset acquisition using the assumed data. However, caution should be taken to review all leasing arrangements and financial justifications with tax counsel.

CHAPTER 11

AN ROI APPROACH
TO MANPOWER EVALUATION

As was previously discussed, capital budgeting can be used successfully for the spending of capital to fulfill capital expenditure requirements for operating a business. If such a concept can be used successfully for capital budgeting, then similar concepts can be used to measure and control human resources or manpower. This concept can then be referred to as return on human capital, return on human resources, or return on human assets. While the original concept of return-on-investment does not change, the definitions of the components and the inputs will have to be redefined. Keep in mind, that most companies do not employ any measure of efficiency in human resources in any calculations in their capital project evaluation process. Remember, employees are probably the most important asset of a company. This method will provide the conceptual framework to evaluate the true costs and the anticipated benefits of a company's human resources. Therefore, one can say that a new way of thinking will be presented about looking at an organization's human resources.

In general, it appears that it is not possible to calculate any meaningful return-on-investment rate for people, even though they are one of the key resources of any organization. One of the reasons for this is that people represent a somewhat unmeasurable asset. In any event, the measurement of employee capabilities such as basic aptitudes, skills, and experience, etc., and an individual's organizational capabilities such as leadership skills, team skills and cooperativeness, tends to be highly judgmental and not subject to quantification. Despite these difficulties, there has been a great deal of time and effort expended in the study of this largely unexplored area. However, most studies fall into the area of productivity and methods for improvement. Such studies concentrate either on cost savings or improved employee morale, such as job enrichment. While much of the studies in this area concentrate on concepts of managing more effectively by such techniques as management by objectives or cost reduction opportunities, it appears that there may be some basis for determining at least a return on some marginal contribution basis.

For example, assuming no change in sales, cost reduction results occur through increases in income, and any reduction in cost can be treated as marginal income for purposes of a return-on-investment calculation. Unfortunately, it is not easy to determine the factors of return-on-investment as was discussed for the capital budgeting process. Some approaches to the investment value include capitalizing the cost of hiring and training of employees, and amortizing these costs over an estimated useful life of the employee based on the assumption, that a lower employee turnover would contribute to a higher return on a company's investment in people.

What Is Human Resource Accounting?

This concept is concerned with capitalizing costs incurred in the training and future development of employees rather than expensing. However, the use of return-on-investment on manpower evaluation will not deal entirely with the human resource accounting mechanism, but rather deal with the basic concepts as it would apply in this case. Under this concept, a portion of the expenses incurred in training and development can be spread and expensed as an employee becomes productive within the organization. If an employee leaves a company, the unamortized or remaining expenses would be written-off to expense and recognized as a loss to the company. This is very similar to depreciating a capital asset, where portions of the capital investment is written-off over the life of the asset in the form of depreciation.

If we look at the mechanics of human resources accounting, there exists several bases by which human resources can be evaluated. They are acquisition, replacement or economic values to a company. Acquisition costs relates to historical transactions necessary to acquire a resource; replacement costs are estimated costs necessary today to replace a resource; and economic values represent the present value of an individual in relation to the contribution to the future earnings of the organization. These bases provide us with the ability to measure the potential earnings ability as to 1) what is the resource cost, 2) what does it now cost, and 3) what its value is. Conceptually, any human resources used during a period in which benefits are derived, are classified as expenses. On the otherhand, any resources used and derived in future periods, are considered assets. It is therefore apparent, that most human resources can be considered assets in the consideration of investments in employees.

The capitalization of costs for human resources can provide a useful tool for managing and developing policies in the hiring practices of an organization. While this concept appears to have more value as an internal management tool, it can be an informative device for reporting the investment to stockholders of human resources and the effect it might have on future earnings of the company. However, there is still some doubt as to the acceptance and/or validity, that this type of reporting would have on the outside community. Such questions as: Can an employee be owned, as an asset is? What is the work life of an employee to determine amortizable costs? Do expenses match revenue during the training and development stage? and What is the personal and social impact will this have on employees? These and many more questions can be raised to argue the pro's and con's of capitalizing employee costs and determining a return-on-investment rate.

Advantages

There are many advantages in using the return-on-investment concept for human resource evaluation. While they are mostly internal reporting advantages, the ultimate rewards will be reflected to the outside community at a later date through higher earnings.

- Determining how to allocate manpower resources in a competing environment.
- Provides a mechanism to use ROI concepts in computing a financial return for measuring human resources.
- Helps in evaluating investment opportunities, that is, manpower vs. capital projects.
- Assists in determining the turnover costs.
- Aides in planning monetary needs in the future for manpower.
- Develops a skill for organization planning, such as promotions, transfers, etc.
- Highlights costs of plant relocations and plant closings.
- Determines the cost of starting up a new plant.
- Evaluates an employee's performance in light of promotion, remain on the job, or dismissal.
- Helps to develop costs attributable to permanent or part-time hires.
- In merger situations, it provides a system for evaluating the management of the company to be acquired.

Disadvantages

- The so-called personnel assets are highly mobile and not owned, and as such, are not in keeping with the traditional definition of assets.
- The possibility of reported earnings manipulation.

- The possible inability to amortize the asset balance on a rational basis once it has been established.
- Employees possibly resenting their treatment as assets.

In summary, there is an anticipation to the company on the impact on profits, on the current value of the human organization, on the current value of the physical resources, and on the current value of the loyalty of customers, suppliers and creditors.

Human Assets vs. Capital Assets

The basic difference between these two assets are that human assets are considered incapable of being transferred. It is probably the most important contribution that management can make to an organization. On the otherhand, capital assets are capable of being sold or transferred to other owners. In addition, accounting practices have allowed companies to write-off the investment in capital assets through depreciation. In human resources, investments can be amortized over the useful life of the employee. If an employee leaves before the end of his estimated useful life, a write-off would occur. It is anticipated that when an employer invests in a new employee, those returns or profits will exceed the costs of employment. An employee's worth can be measured by two interrelated variables, that is, the expected life or tenure with the company and the contributions over that expected period.

In comparing to a capital project, an expected life of an employee can be varied, unlike a capital project which is more definitely fixed. Employees can voluntarily or involuntarily be dismissed from the organization. Therefore, it is recommended that shorter evaluations be initiated such as two and five year evaluations, as compared to longer evaluations for capital projects. It is also important to reassess an employee after five years to evaluate past performance, and project performance for the next five year period.

Methods For Measuring The Value of Human Resources

- *Return on Effort Employed* — a point value is given to the job title (i.e., 1 point for a clerk up to 10 for the president or chairman of the board) and this is multiplied by a personal assessment factor and multiplied again by a factor based on length of employment (i.e., 1-2 years, 1.1, up to 4 years, 1.2, etc.). The overall figure could be divided by total profits to determine the return rate.

- *Cost Approach* – measures an investment in manpower similar to the capital expenditures investment concept. Such costs as hiring, recruiting, transportation costs, training and development, etc., can be totalled and amortization schedules compiled and expensed to the earnings statement as utilized. An additional approach reflects current replacement costs and considers the manpower investment beyond the historical costs of obtaining employees. This method assumes a current value of replacing employees of equal qualifications and tends to reflect inflationary trends by providing an up-to-date cost estimate for both turnover costs and long-range manpower planning.
- *Value Approach* – relates the value of the human resources as a function of the wages or profits of the company. For example, that part of future profits which differs from industry averages could provide the basis for establishing the value of human resources in terms of investment return on human resources. A more sophisticated approach establishes the estimated costs of present and future wage payments and develops a current return on human resources ratio to forecasted future profits. The result is then compared to the industry rate, and the difference representing the value of the human organization.
- *Economic Approach* – suggests that the value of an employee is based on the marketplace. That is, the supply and demand factors in which competitive bidding takes place whereby the employer bidding the highest price, usually hires the services of the employee. Therefore, the value of the employee is the price needed to obtain the services of the employee.
- *Goodwill Method* – earnings in excess of an industry average would be calculated and then a proportion of this would be attributed to human factors.
- *Behavorial Variables Method* – would involve statistical analyses of variations in leadership ability correlated with increases in profits, productivity and other income factors. This would seem to depend on subjective evaluations despite the mathematics.

Costs of Human Resources

The investments made for human resources take many different forms which are reflected in the earnings of the company. For example, out-of-pocket expenditures for activities such as recruiting and acquisition, training and development, and allocating salaries during training and development periods. We can suggest those expenses which can be capitalized as assets, be included on the balance sheet, and those as expenses, be included on the earnings statement. Keep in mind, that these categories may not meet the standards as presented by the accounting profession, but nevertheless, can be a valuable tool for internal evaluation.

Costs of Human Resources
Expense Classifications

Salaries & Wages
Salaries
Commissions
Overrides
Bonuses
Overtime
Payroll Taxes
  Social Security
  State and Federal Taxes
  Unemployment Compensation

Benefits
Group Life Insurance
Accident and Health Plans
Pension Plan Contributions
Profit Sharing Plans
Stock Plans
Travel Insurance
Supplies
Amortization
Write-Offs

Asset Classifications

Professional Development – costs used to increase an employee's capabilities in skills training and organizational development beyond what is needed in the current position.
Seminar Fees
Continuing Education
– Outside
– Inside
Professional Dues and Fees
Professional Meeting and
Travel Expenses

Recruiting Costs – costs involved in locating and selecting new personnel.
Employment Advertising
Interviewing Expenses
– External
– Internal (includes time spent by other departments)
Testing and Evaluation
Search Fees

Acquisition Costs – costs used to acquire a new employee to a point where the employee becomes operational
Fees to Employment Agencies and Search Firms
Medical Examination Fees
Moving Costs
Time Spent in Administering Paper Work to Hire Employees
Cost of Initial Supplies Needed to Perform Job

Training – costs incurred immediately after employment
On-the-job Training
Orientation
Costs of Other Employee Including Salary Allocations
Costs of Integrating New Employees Such as Philosophy, History, Policies, Objectives, Communication Lines, Reporting Relationships, etc.

Measurement Techniques

Since this concept is still in the early stages of development, many different methods can be employed in reaching its objectives, with no one method having an advantage over another. However, each company must evaluate its needs and objectives and choose the one method, or adaptation of several, in reaching the agreed upon method of measuring human resources.

Measuring Staff Personnel

Utilizing the original formula of return-on-investment, that is, the profitability rate times the turnover rate, this formula can be used to measure staff personnel by applying the following formula:

$$\frac{\text{Job Earnings}}{\text{Net Sales}} \times \frac{\text{MBO Job Value}}{\text{Insurance Value}}$$

Three new terms are introduced, namely, job earnings, MBO job value, and insurance value. These terms are defined as follows:

Job Earnings

This is the calculation of MBO Job Value less the discounted cash flow of salary, training and related employee benefits. To such items as actual salary, bonuses, and monetized benefits, cash flows are added to return such items as hiring costs and training over a specific period of time at a specific opportunity cost. The opportunity cost represents a desired rate of return. The discounted cash flow calculation is the total payment to keep an employee in his job.

MBO Job Value

This is the value of a job as measured through a management by objectives (MBO) process. The staff employee and his immediate superior agree to certain objectives to be reached over the next year. These objectives are then measured as to the employee's worth to the company. Thus, the calculation of Job Earnings/MBO Job Value indicates the productivity of the employee. If the employee is earning more than the worth of the calculated objective, then the equation of MBO Job Value less DCF will be equal to, or less than, zero. With a zero or negative numerator, the productivity ratio will be zero or negative.

Insurance Value

The total value or assets of the employee can be defined as to what amount a company is willing to insure an employee. Thus, the calculation could be the aggregate of an employee's salary, benefits, training and development, hiring costs, cost of replacement, and corporate property value. The value of the staff employee to the company is the total value, and not just the yearly or MBO Job Value. If the employee increases productivity by setting and reaching higher MBO objectives, then achievement of a greater and shorter turnover of assets results. At this point, the insurance value should probably be increased to bring the ratio back into line. For example, a ratio of over 50%, suggests that the employee should be scheduled for further training to enhance the job. If the ratio falls below 10%, then training of a remedial nature may be suggested. These ratio levels are for illustration purposes only, and a company should develop its own standards. It is well to note, that no attempt is made to minimize the problems of measuring the worth or MBO Job Value of an employee, since many other subjective items must be considered such as keeping family control of the business, and special forms of compensation.

Measuring Professional Service Firms

One type of organization that seems to be more adaptable to the use of return-on-investment, is the professional service firm. These would include law firms, CPA firms, and consulting firms. The assumption is that the firms can reasonably forecast the demand for their services, and based on this, the firm can calculate a return-on-investment rate of a new employee. The calculation will be based on the previously mentioned calculation of return on controllable assets. The computation is as follows:

$$\frac{\text{Marginal Contribution}}{\text{Net Billings}} \times \frac{\text{Net Billings}}{\text{Controllable Assets}}$$

or

$$\frac{\text{Marginal Contribution}}{\text{Controllable Assets}}$$

Marginal Contribution
Both marginal contribution and net billings will be illustrated by using the following example.

Estimate of chargeable hours	2,000 hours
X	
Billing rate of new hire	$50/hour
equals	
Gross billings	$100,000
Less: Allowance for uncollectable accounts	5,000
Net billings	95,000

Less: Salary, employee benefits, and other variable training costs	35,000
Marginal contribution	$ 60,000

Controllable Assets

For a professional firm, this represents accounts receivable and work-in-process (that is, time charged to a particular client(s), but not yet billed).

Illustration

Accounts receivable	$40,000
Work-in-process	35,000
Controllable assets	$75,000

Return on Controllable Assets

$$\frac{\text{Marginal Contribution}}{\text{Net Billings}} \times \frac{\text{Net Billings}}{\text{Controllable Assets}}$$

or

$$\frac{\$60,000}{\$95,000} \times \frac{\$95,000}{\$75,000}$$

$$63.16\% \times 1.2667$$

Return on Controllable Assets = 80%

Overall Impact

Return-on-investment performance relates to a combination of volume performance, cost control and asset utilization, all of which are related to people to the degree which they do or do not perform their task and their attitude while doing it. Since each portion of the ROI equation is essentially people related, any policy or system which enhances a company's utilization of its employees will have a direct bearing upon the attaining of company goals.

To reflect the overall impact to the company of expenditures for training and development, the following financial statements are presented. You will note that the earnings statement includes an identifiable amount for human resource investment. In addition, the balance sheet reflects not only the asset investment in human resources, but deferrals of federal income taxes as a result of appropriations for human resources, and an apportionment of retained earn-

ings for human resource appropriations. Both financial statements show the
impact of reflecting investments in human resources (Financial and Human
Resource heading) as compared to the traditional financial statement (Financial
heading).

Earnings Statement

	Financial and Human Resource	Financial
Net Sales	$1,500,000	$1,500,000
Cost of Goods Sold	1,250,000	1,250,000
Gross Profit	250,000	250,000
Less: Selling, General and		
Administrative Expenses	55,000	55,000
Depreciation	20,000	20,000
Net Operating Income	175,000	175,000
Other Income – Net	5,000	5,000
Net Before Income Tax	180,000	180,000
Net Increase (Decrease) in		
Human Resource Investment	(3,000)	–
Adjusted Income Before Tax	177,000	180,000
Income Tax	88,500	90,000
Net Earnings	$ 88,500	$ 90,000

Balance Sheet

	Financial and Human Resource	Financial
Assets		
Total Current Assets	$400,000	$400,000
Net Plant and Equipment	500,000	500,000
Net Investments in		
Human Resources	60,000	–
Total Assets	$960,000	$900,000

Liabilities and Stockholders'
  Equity

Total Current Liabilities	$200,000	$200,000
Long-Term Debt	250,000	250,000
Deferred Federal Income Taxes as a Result of Appropriation for Human Resources	30,000	–
Stockholders' Equity	300,000	300,000
Retained Earnings:		
Financial	150,000	150,000
Appropriation for Human Resources	30,000	–
Total Liabilities and Stockholders' Equity	$960,000	$900,000

Ratio Comparisons

Many comparisons can be made which will act as an indicator for measuring performance. Like all ratios, they are merely management tools, and should be used with other acceptable tools of management.

Human Assets to Total Assets

The human asset investment ratio is a useful indicator of future profit performance. A correlation exists between the profitability of a company and the training and development costs associated with human resources. A higher ratio suggests potential higher profits, conversely, a lower ratio suggests potentially lower profits.

Calculation

$$\frac{\text{Human Assets}}{\text{Total Assets}} = \frac{\$\ 60,000}{\$960,000} = 6.25\%$$

Return on Total Assets

Applying the return on total asset concept, the impact of investments in human assets is clearly reflected. In previous illustrations, the return on total assets was 10.0% computed as follows:

$$\frac{\text{Net Earnings}}{\text{Net Sales}} \times \frac{\text{Net Sales}}{\text{Total Assets}}$$

or

$$\frac{\text{Profitability}}{\text{Rate}} \times \frac{\text{Turnover}}{\text{Rate}}$$

$$\frac{\$\ \ 90,000}{\$1,500,000} \times \frac{\$1,500,000}{\$\ \ 900,000} = 10.0\%$$

$$6\% \times 1.667 = 10.0\%$$

With human resource investments added, the return on total assets is 9.2%.

$$\frac{\text{Net Earnings}}{\text{Net Sales}} \times \frac{\text{Net Sales}}{\text{Total Assets}}$$

or

$$\frac{\text{Profitability}}{\text{Rate}} \times \frac{\text{Turnover}}{\text{Rate}}$$

$$\frac{\$\ \ 88,500}{\$1,500,000} \times \frac{\$1,500,000}{\$\ \ 960,000} = 9.2\%$$

$$5.9\% \times 1.5625 = 9.2\%$$

Viewed this way, the impact of human resources exhibits a lower ROI, both in the profitability rate and the turnover rate. What is not measured in this calculation, is the affect of this type of presentation on the employees and the programs affecting them.

Summary

It is clear that many companies are currently using increasingly sophisticated techniques to measure the value of their employees and there will be increasing pressure on the government to allow them to capitalize such costs. For example, in certain defense contracts, tax courts have held that the cost of obtaining certain types of engineering talent could be put in the investment base. The idea of ROI is to make the measurement as accurate and inclusive as possible, and obviously, it is presently being distorted when costs of training programs are put in as an expense in one year while the return comes back in the future. On the otherhand, critical decisions should be made on relative ROI's rather than absolute ones. Given a situation where two companies in an industry have similar employee programs, the present measurements should give an accurate relationship between them. This is the narrow view, and no doubt, there are great differences between programs costing the same. The main value of this concept would be in the larger view which measures actual present values of people. None of the methods mentioned are perfect and most would have to be refined over many years of use before they could be accepted in a company's financial reporting. If a proper program of measurement is installed, it could more than offset its cost of implementation in the value of both the individual and the management knowing what the results are. An ineffective plan could cause employee unrest and easily cost more than the value of the benefits of more accurate ROI indexes. In summary, this concept can be of extreme value to managing a company, since it puts a cost value on personnel decisions which previously were largely subjective in nature.

CHAPTER 12

OTHER USES
AND APPLICATIONS

MAPI

The Machinery and Allied Products Institute pioneered a method of evaluating capital investments which is referred to as the MAPI method. This method was developed for evaluating capital replacements. The MAPI method determines a rate of return over a specific time period for each proposed investment relative to the alternative of maintaining the existing method of operation. The rate of return measures the urgency of an investment today as compared to a later period in time and is referred to as the "urgency rating." Investments can be ranked according to their urgency rating. The general rule is applied to the ﹨urgency rating whereby those investments with the highest ratings, would be more important to replace immediately rather than any deferment. Therefore, those investments showing the highest urgency rating would be selected. Some of the drawbacks of this method are as follows:

- Considerable amount of data is required beyond the typical data necessary to a capital investment proposal.
- Tendency for results to yield a higher rate of return when compared to other capital investment techniques.
- Even more academic and sophisticated than DCF techniques.
- Harder to understand.
- Favors larger industries, particularly those that sell capital equipment.

Computation

The formula for computation of the MAPI method is as follows:

Operating advantage plus capital consumption avoided by the investment, minus capital consumption incurred, minus income tax adjustments, divided by the average net investment.

The operating advantage represents the net increase in revenues due to changes in quality of products and changes in volume of output, less the net decrease in operating costs resulting from the project. Capital consumption avoided is the calculation of the decline in value of the disposal value of the investment if it were not to be disposed of during the measurement period. Capital consumption incurred measures the decline in value which the investment would incur over the measurement period. Income tax adjustments represent actual income taxes payable. Average net investment reflects the average incremental investment for the period.

ESTIMATING A PURCHASE PRICE FOR AN ACQUISTION

Companies can be acquired through the issuance of stock, cash, long-term financing or a combination of several or possibly all of these arrangements. The price of an acquisition can be established based on the multiple of earnings, premium over book value in exchange for stock or other assets, or any other mutually agreed upon price. As you can see, determining the purchase price to pay or to offer can be a problem. In many cases, there is an agreement based on the intuition and judgment of the parties involved during negotiation. It is therefore obvious, that there is no one way of computing a price, or in fact, a correct price. However, one way to approach the problem of estimating a purchase price is to use discounted cash flow techniques. These techniques were explored in earlier chapters, but presents a less sophisticated method in computing the acquisition purchase price.

For example, assuming Company A is interested in acquiring Company B and decides to make an offer. Under the DCF techniques, a determined target is established for which Company A has chosen 20%. This target rate is the minimum rate Company A would accept, which is based on the company's overall return-on-investment objective. This means that Company A would not want to acquire Company B unless it returned at least 20%, but preferably higher than 20%. However, this may not be true when other significant factors not relating to profits make an acquisition desirable.

The basic disadvantage of using this method is that it relies heavily upon estimated projections, in which the margin of error is undeterminable. Assuming that the financial projections are reasonable, the following facts are presented for Company B estimating the future net sales, net earnings, depreciation, and incremental working capital for an eight year period, resulting in projected net cash flows.

Assumptions
Average Growth of Net Sales — 10%
Net Earnings — 6% of Net Sales
Incremental Working Capital — 20% of incremental net sales

Company B
Estimated Net Cash Flows
($ in thousands)

	Year 1	Year 2	Year 3	Year 4
Net Sales	$ 8,000	$ 8,800	$ 9,680	$10,648
Net Earnings	480	528	581	639
Depreciation	35	43	30	25
Cash Flows	515	571	611	664
Less: Incremental				
Working Capital	900	160	176	194
Net Cash Flows	(385)	411	435	470
Cumulative Net				
Cash Flows	($385)	$ 26	$ 461	$ 931

	Year 5	Year 6	Year 7	Year 8
Net Sales	$11,713	$12,884	$14,172	$15,589
Net Earnings	703	773	850	935
Depreciation	30	20	18	15
Cash Flows	733	793	868	950
Less: Incremental				
Working Capital	213	234	258	283
Net Cash Flows	520	559	610	667
Cumulative Net				
Cash Flows	$ 1,451	$ 2,010	$ 2,620	$ 3,287

To determine the purchase price, the net cash flows will be discounted at the established minimum target rate of 20%.

Company B
Calculation Of The Purchase Price
($ in thousands)

Year	Net Cash Flows	Discount Factor @ 20%	Discounted Cash Flows
1	($ 385)	.83333	($ 321)
2	411	.69444	285
3	435	.57870	252
4	470	.48225	227
5	520	.40188	209
6	559	.33490	187
7	610	.27908	170
8	667	.23257	155
Total	$3,287		$1,164

The discounted purchase price at 20% target rate is $1,164,000.

EVALUATING ENERGY CONSERVATION

As we saw in earlier chapters, any investment that derives greater benefits than costs, could be considered a sound investment, assuming it added incremental profit to the business. This same concept can apply to energy conservation. Under this concept, benefits can be obtained by little more than operational changes that can be made at minimal cost without sacrificing any product quality. Many of these opportunities may require additional capital outlay's, and in a period of rapid rises in energy costs, economic justification can be made for any monies spent on these projects. These additional capital outlay's for energy conservation opportunities can be amortized by the energy savings generated over their expected lifetime. We will deal with some of the capital investment concepts, namely, payback and internal rate of return for evaluating energy conservation.

Like capital investment opportunities, developing quantitative data for measuring energy opportunities with alternative investment opportunities is also important. Since the true economic cost includes opportunity costs of foregone investments, energy conservation opportunities should be considered profitable, only when their expected rate of return is greater than that which could be realized from other alternative investment opportunities.

Many energy conservation opportunities may be found during a close examination of operations, but may be rejected due to an unfavorable return-on-investment or a longer than expected payback period. Without recapping the pro's and con's of these techniques which were discussed earlier, the data necessary to calculate these concepts are as follows:

ECO = Energy Conservation Opportunities
FC = First Cost
AOC = Annual Operating Cost
AFS = Annual Fuel Savings
PFP = Projected Fuel Price
EL = Estimated Lifetime

The first cost is the estimated dollar cost of labor and materials necessary to implement the project. The AOC, AFS, PFP and EL will determine the annual benefits, excluding any salvage value of the investment. Therefore, the net annual savings can be defined by the following equation.

$$\text{Net Annual Savings (S)} = (\text{AFS} \times \text{PFP}) - \text{AOC}$$

Payback Period

The payback period is calculated by dividing the first cost by the net annual savings.

$$\text{Payback Period} = \frac{\text{FC}}{(\text{AFS} \times \text{PFP}) - \text{AOC}}$$

or

$$\text{Payback Period} = \frac{\text{FC}}{\text{S}}$$

The payback period is then compared to the expected lifetime (EL) of the investment to determine the approximate recovery of the investment. A payback period of less than one-half the lifetime of an investment would generally be considered profitable where the lifetime is ten years or less. Keep in mind the disadvantages that exists in the payback period method which also applies in this application (refer to payback methods).

Return-on-Investment Concept

Applying the return-on-investment concept, the depletion of the investment over its economic life is accounted for through depreciation charges (DC). Using the depreciation charge, the calculation is:

$$DC = \frac{FC}{EL}$$

which relates to the return-on-investment as follows:

$$ROI = \frac{S - DC}{FC} \times 100\%$$

Other Measurement Techniques

Other measurement techniques are available which supplements the previous two methods. They are the benefit/cost analysis, the time to recoup capital investment and the internal rate of return.

Benefit/Cost Analysis

This method requires the direct comparison of the present value benefits (savings) generated by a given investment with its costs and is referred to as the benefit/cost ratio. A ratio greater than one implies that the expected net benefits (after discounting) will exceed the initial costs and therefore, considered to be profitable. A benefit/cost ratio less than one implies that an investment will not be profitable.

Time To Recoup Capital Investment

This concept is similar to the payback period method except that discount rates are taken into consideration.

Discounted Cash Flows (DCF)

This concept uses discounting in arriving at what rate the discounted cash flows equal zero. The following table will be used for discounting calculations.

Discount Table

@ 15%

Year (EL)	Cumulative Discount Rate (D)	Year (EL)	Cumulative Discount Rate (D)
1	0.86957	6	3.78449
2	1.62571	7	4.16043
3	2.28323	8	4.48733
4	2.85498	9	4.77159
5	3.35216	10	5.01877

Note: This table is calculated from the following equation:

$$PV = \frac{1 - (1+D)^{-EL}}{D}$$

Illustration

The following is an illustration of a company considering a capital investment in the manufacturing process for energy conservation purposes. The following facts will be used:

Assumptions

Cost of Design and Installation — $400,000
Average Savings — 100,000 MBtu of natural gas per year
Estimated Lifetime — Ten years
Average Cost of Fuel — $3.50 per MBtu
Objective Rate — 15%

Based on the above assumptions, will this be a profitable investment?

$$\text{Net Annual Savings (S)} = (\text{AFS} \times \text{PFP}) - \text{AOC}$$
$$S = 100,000 \times \$3.50 - 0$$
$$S = \$350,000 \text{ per year}$$

$$\text{Payback Period (PP)} = \frac{FC}{S}$$

$$PP = \frac{\$400,000}{\$350,000} = 1.14 \text{ years}$$

Return-on-Investment

$$DC = \frac{FC}{EL}$$

$$DC = \frac{\$400,000}{10} = \$40,000 \text{ per year}$$

$$ROI = \frac{S - DC}{FC} \times 100\%$$

$$ROI = \frac{\$350,000 - \$40,000}{\$400,000} \times 100\%$$

$$ROI = 77.5\% \text{ per year}$$

Based on return-on-investment, this appears to be an attractive investment.

Benefit/Cost Analysis

To arrive at this ratio, the present value (PV) of the future savings must be calculated for a 15% discount (D) for 10 years (EL). The present value of the net annual savings (S) is:

PV = S X PV
PV = $350,000 X 5.01877
PV = $1,756,570

This results in a benefit/cost ratio (B/C) of 4.39 as follows:

$$B/C = \frac{PV}{FC}$$

$$B/C = \frac{\$1,756,570}{\$\ 400,000}$$

$$B/C = 4.39$$

This investment can be considered profitable even after discounting.

Time to Recoup Investment

This can be approximated by referring to the discount table and relating the earlier calculation of the payback period which resulted in 1.14 years. The number coming closest to 1.14 years is 1.62571 which indicates that the investment will be entirely recouped in about 2 years considering the time value of money. While this is longer than the original payback period of 1.14 years without discounting, it does provide a better indication of the profitability of this investment because it includes opportunity costs. If the correct discount rate were used, any investment which is recouped in a period less than its lifetime, should be considered profitable.

RETURN-ON-INVESTMENT IN INVENTORY CONTROL

Successful businesses spend a great deal of time in controlling inventory levels, as evidenced by the many inventory control systems that are present in today's business environment. In addition, since inventory contributes a sizable percent to the overall investment of a company, proper control is essential to keep inventory levels at a minimum level for effective and less costly operations. Too often, businesses measure inventory as a measurement of turnover ratios. While this yardstick measures the speed of which inventories are passed through

105

the business, the effect on profits are completely ignored. The standard premise of the faster the turnover, the higher the return, is not necessarily a true and accurate statement.

As we saw in earlier chapters, increased return-on-investment can be increased by changes in the turnover rate, of which inventories are a major part. While inventory control systems are a means of inventory evaluation, it is suggested that inventory objectives should include maximizing return-on-investment in inventories. However, like all measurable yardsticks, this method of inventory control does not strive for perfection, but merely a sound and practical approach. Like any practical approach, we must face the realities involved in the evaluation process, such as the inventory control process.

Utilizing the basic equation of earnings divided by investment, we can apply this principle to test the effectiveness of additional inventory on the return-on-investment equation. This is done by estimating the incremental earnings and incremental inventory amounts and apply it to the formula. Simply, if $100,000 additional inventory generates earnings of $10,000, the incremental return-on-investment would be 10%. You can reach the conclusion of what additional inventory investments and earnings will have as an increment, as well as the effect on the overall company, by applying this increment to the overall amounts. This is only one tool for improving return-on-investment, and it is not to be construed as a panacea for all inventory problems.

USING ROI TO ESTABLISH PRICES

The pricing decision can rest with many parts of the organization. It can rest with the President, Executive Vice President, Division President, or any other level of management having profit responsibility. While it is recognized that pricing should lead to a profit objective, many pricing decisions are based on competitive conditions which may dictate the price of a product. Assuming that some flexibility exists, pricing can be determined by utilizing the time value of money (discounting) as follows:

Assumptions

Investment in Product	$500,000
Production Costs	300,000
Selling, General and Administrative Expenses	90,000
Desired Return-on-Investment	20%
Annual Unit Production	50,000 units
Tax Rate	50%
Estimated Life	10 years

The annual net earnings required to produce a 20% return-on-investment rate is $100,000 ($500,000 X .20). With the tax rate at 50%, the before tax earnings would be $200,000. To this, we add production costs ($300,000), selling, general and administrative expenses ($90,000), and straight-line depreciation of $50,000 ($500,000/10). Therefore, the net sales required would be $640,000 ($200,000 + $300,000 + $90,000 + $50,000).

The unit sales price would be $12.80 ($640,000/50,000). This is proven by the following calculation.

Annual Unit Production — 50,000 units at $12.80	$640,000
Less: Production Costs	300,000
	340,000
Less: Depreciation	50,000
Selling, General and Administrative Expenses	90,000
Profit Before Taxes	200,000
Taxes at 50%	100,000
Net Earnings	$100,000
Investment	$500,000
20% Desired Return-on-Investment	$100,000

Therefore, to achieve a 20% desired ROI, the product would have to be priced at $12.80, assuming the above facts.

APPENDIX

Tables

Appendix A

Present Value Tables

Years	1%	2%	4%	6%	8%	10%	12%	14%
1	0.990	0.980	0.962	0.943	0.926	0.909	0.893	0.877
2	0.980	0.961	0.925	0.890	0.857	0.826	0.797	0.769
3	0.971	0.942	0.889	0.840	0.794	0.751	0.712	0.675
4	0.961	0.924	0.855	0.792	0.735	0.683	0.636	0.592
5	0.951	0.906	0.822	0.747	0.681	0.621	0.567	0.519
6	0.942	0.888	0.790	0.705	0.630	0.564	0.507	0.456
7	0.933	0.871	0.760	0.665	0.583	0.513	0.452	0.400
8	0.923	0.853	0.731	0.627	0.540	0.467	0.404	0.351
9	0.914	0.837	0.703	0.592	0.500	0.424	0.361	0.308
10	0.905	0.820	0.676	0.558	0.463	0.386	0.322	0.270
11	0.896	0.804	0.650	0.527	0.429	0.350	0.287	0.237
12	0.887	0.788	0.625	0.497	0.397	0.319	0.257	0.208
13	0.879	0.773	0.601	0.469	0.368	0.290	0.229	0.182
14	0.870	0.758	0.577	0.442	0.340	0.263	0.205	0.160
15	0.861	0.743	0.555	0.417	0.315	0.239	0.183	0.140
16	0.853	0.728	0.534	0.394	0.292	0.218	0.163	0.123
17	0.844	0.714	0.513	0.371	0.270	0.198	0.146	0.108
18	0.836	0.700	0.494	0.350	0.250	0.180	0.130	0.095
19	0.828	0.686	0.475	0.331	0.232	0.164	0.116	0.083
20	0.820	0.673	0.456	0.312	0.215	0.149	0.104	0.073
21	0.811	0.660	0.439	0.294	0.199	0.135	0.093	0.064
22	0.803	0.647	0.422	0.278	0.184	0.123	0.083	0.056
23	0.795	0.634	0.406	0.262	0.170	0.112	0.074	0.049
24	0.788	0.622	0.390	0.247	0.158	0.102	0.066	0.043
25	0.780	0.610	0.375	0.233	0.146	0.092	0.059	0.038
26	0.772	0.598	0.361	0.220	0.135	0.084	0.053	0.033
27	0.764	0.586	0.347	0.207	0.125	0.076	0.047	0.029
28	0.757	0.574	0.333	0.196	0.116	0.069	0.042	0.026
29	0.749	0.563	0.321	0.185	0.107	0.063	0.037	0.022
30	0.742	0.552	0.308	0.174	0.099	0.057	0.033	0.020

Present Value Tables (Continued)

Years	15%	16%	18%	20%	22%	24%	25%	26%
1	0.870	0.862	0.847	0.833	0.820	0.806	0.800	0.794
2	0.756	0.743	0.718	0.694	0.672	0.650	0.640	0.630
3	0.658	0.641	0.609	0.579	0.551	0.524	0.512	0.500
4	0.572	0.552	0.516	0.482	0.451	0.423	0.410	0.397
5	0.497	0.476	0.437	0.402	0.370	0.341	0.328	0.315
6	0.432	0.410	0.370	0.335	0.303	0.275	0.262	0.250
7	0.376	0.354	0.314	0.279	0.249	0.222	0.210	0.198
8	0.327	0.305	0.266	0.233	0.204	0.179	0.168	0.157
9	0.284	0.263	0.225	0.194	0.167	0.144	0.134	0.125
10	0.247	0.227	0.191	0.162	0.137	0.116	0.107	0.099
11	0.215	0.195	0.162	0.135	0.112	0.094	0.086	0.079
12	0.187	0.168	0.137	0.112	0.092	0.076	0.069	0.062
13	0.163	0.145	0.116	0.093	0.075	0.061	0.055	0.050
14	0.141	0.125	0.099	0.078	0.062	0.049	0.044	0.039
15	0.123	0.108	0.084	0.065	0.051	0.040	0.035	0.031
16	0.107	0.093	0.071	0.054	0.042	0.032	0.028	0.025
17	0.093	0.080	0.060	0.045	0.034	0.026	0.023	0.020
18	0.081	0.069	0.051	0.038	0.028	0.021	0.018	0.016
19	0.070	0.060	0.043	0.031	0.023	0.017	0.014	0.012
20	0.061	0.051	0.037	0.026	0.019	0.014	0.012	0.010
21	0.053	0.044	0.031	0.022	0.015	0.011	0.009	0.008
22	0.046	0.038	0.026	0.018	0.013	0.009	0.007	0.006
23	0.040	0.033	0.022	0.015	0.010	0.007	0.006	0.005
24	0.035	0.028	0.019	0.013	0.008	0.006	0.005	0.004
25	0.030	0.024	0.016	0.010	0.007	0.005	0.004	0.003
26	0.026	0.021	0.014	0.009	0.006	0.004	0.003	0.002
27	0.023	0.018	0.011	0.007	0.005	0.003	0.002	0.002
28	0.020	0.016	0.010	0.006	0.004	0.002	0.002	0.002
29	0.017	0.014	0.008	0.005	0.003	0.002	0.002	0.001
30	0.015	0.012	0.007	0.004	0.003	0.002	0.001	0.001

Present Value Tables (Continued)

Years	28%	30%	35%	40%	45%	50%
1	0.781	0.769	0.741	0.714	0.690	0.667
2	0.610	0.592	0.549	0.510	0.476	0.444
3	0.477	0.455	0.406	0.364	0.328	0.296
4	0.373	0.350	0.301	0.260	0.226	0.198
5	0.291	0.269	0.223	0.186	0.156	0.132
6	0.227	0.207	0.165	0.133	0.108	0.088
7	0.178	0.159	0.122	0.095	0.074	0.059
8	0.139	0.123	0.091	0.068	0.051	0.039
9	0.108	0.094	0.067	0.048	0.035	0.026
10	0.085	0.073	0.050	0.035	0.024	0.017
11	0.066	0.056	0.037	0.025	0.017	0.012
12	0.052	0.043	0.027	0.018	0.012	0.008
13	0.040	0.033	0.020	0.013	0.008	0.005
14	0.032	0.025	0.015	0.009	0.006	0.003
15	0.025	0.020	0.011	0.006	0.004	0.002
16	0.019	0.015	0.008	0.005	0.003	0.002
17	0.015	0.012	0.006	0.003	0.002	0.001
18	0.012	0.009	0.005	0.002	0.001	0.001
19	0.009	0.007	0.003	0.002	0.001	
20	0.007	0.005	0.002	0.001	0.001	
21	0.006	0.004	0.002	0.001		
22	0.004	0.003	0.001	0.001		
23	0.003	0.002	0.001			
24	0.003	0.002	0.001			
25	0.002	0.001	0.001			
26	0.002	0.001				
27	0.001	0.001				
28	0.001	0.001				
29	0.001	0.001				
30	0.001					

Appendix B

Compound Tables

Year	1%	2%	3%	4%	5%	6%	7%
1	1.010	1.020	1.030	1.040	1.050	1.060	1.070
2	1.020	1.040	1.061	1.082	1.102	1.124	1.145
3	1.030	1.061	1.093	1.125	1.156	1.191	1.225
4	1.041	1.082	1.126	1.170	1.216	1.262	1.311
5	1.051	1.104	1.159	1.217	1.276	1.338	1.403
6	1.062	1.120	1.194	1.265	1.340	1.419	1.501
7	1.072	1.149	1.230	1.316	1.407	1.504	1.606
8	1.083	1.172	1.267	1.369	1.477	1.594	1.718
9	1.094	1.195	1.305	1.423	1.551	1.689	1.838
10	1.105	1.219	1.344	1.480	1.629	1.791	1.967
11	1.116	1.243	1.384	1.539	1.710	1.898	2.105
12	1.127	1.268	1.426	1.601	1.796	2.012	2.252
13	1.138	1.294	1.469	1.665	1.886	2.133	2.410
14	1.149	1.319	1.513	1.732	1.980	2.261	2.579
15	1.161	1.346	1.558	1.801	2.079	2.397	2.759
16	1.173	1.373	1.605	1.873	2.183	2.540	2.952
17	1.184	1.400	1.653	1.948	2.292	2.693	3.159
18	1.196	1.428	1.702	2.026	2.407	2.854	3.380
19	1.208	1.457	1.754	2.107	2.527	3.026	3.617
20	1.220	1.486	1.806	2.191	2.653	3.207	3.870
25	1.282	1.641	2.094	2.666	3.386	4.292	5.427
30	1.348	1.811	2.427	3.243	4.322	5.743	7.612

Compound Tables (Continued)

Year	8%	9%	10%	12%	14%	15%	16%
1	1.080	1.090	1.100	1.120	1.140	1.150	1.160
2	1.166	1.188	1.210	1.254	1.300	1.322	1.346
3	1.260	1.295	1.331	1.405	1.482	1.521	1.561
4	1.360	1.412	1.464	1.574	1.689	1.749	1.811
5	1.469	1.539	1.611	1.762	1.925	2.011	2.100
6	1.587	1.677	1.772	1.974	2.195	2.313	2.436
7	1.714	1.828	1.949	2.211	2.502	2.660	2.826
8	1.851	1.993	2.144	2.476	2.853	3.059	3.278
9	1.999	2.172	2.358	2.773	3.252	3.518	3.803
10	2.159	2.367	2.594	3.106	3.707	4.046	4.411
11	2.332	2.580	2.853	3.479	4.226	4.652	5.117
12	2.518	2.813	3.138	3.896	4.818	5.350	5.936
13	2.720	3.066	3.452	4.363	5.492	6.153	6.886
14	2.937	3.342	3.797	4.887	6.261	7.076	7.988
15	3.172	3.642	4.177	5.474	7.138	8.137	9.266
16	3.426	3.970	4.595	6.130	8.137	9.358	10.748
17	3.700	4.328	5.054	6.866	9.276	10.761	12.468
18	3.996	4.717	5.560	7.690	10.575	12.375	14.463
19	4.316	5.142	6.116	8.613	12.056	14.232	16.777
20	4.661	5.604	6.728	9.646	13.743	16.367	19.461
25	6.848	8.632	10.835	17.000	26.462	32.919	40.874
30	10.063	13.268	17.449	29.960	50.950	66.212	85.850

Compound Tables (Continued)

Year	18%	20%	24%	28%	32%	40%	50%
1	1.180	1.200	1.240	1.280	1.320	1.400	1.500
2	1.392	1.440	1.538	1.638	1.742	1.960	2.250
3	1.643	1.728	1.907	2.067	2.300	2.744	3.375
4	1.939	2.074	2.364	2.684	3.036	3.842	5.062
5	2.288	2.488	2.932	3.436	4.007	5.378	7.594
6	2.700	2.986	3.635	4.398	5.290	7.530	11.391
7	3.185	3.583	4.508	5.629	6.983	10.541	17.086
8	3.759	4.300	5.590	7.206	9.217	14.758	25.629
9	4.435	5.160	6.931	9.223	12.166	20.661	38.443
10	5.234	6.192	8.594	11.806	16.060	28.925	57.665
11	6.176	7.430	10.657	15.112	21.199	40.496	86.498
12	7.288	8.916	13.215	19.343	27.983	56.694	129.746
13	8.599	10.699	16.386	24.759	36.937	79.372	194.619
14	10.147	12.839	20.319	31.691	48.757	111.120	291.929
15	11.074	15.407	25.196	40.565	64.350	155.568	437.894
16	14.129	18.488	31.243	51.923	84.954	217.795	656.84
17	16.672	22.186	38.741	66.461	112.14	304.914	985.26
18	19.673	26.623	48.039	85.071	148.02	426.879	1477.9
19	23.214	31.948	59.568	108.89	195.39	597.630	2216.8
20	27.393	38.338	73.864	139.38	257.92	836.683	3325.3
25	62.669	95.396	216.542	478.90	1033.6	4499.880	25251.
30	143.371	237.376	634.820	1645.5	4142.1	24201.432	191750.

GLOSSARY

accelerated depreciation method Sum-of-the-years'-digits and double-declining methods.

accounting method Measures capital investments by conventional methods of generally accepted accounting principles in recording income and investments.

accounting rate of return See Accounting Method.

acid test ratio Supplements the current ratio by placing emphasis on liquid assets which can be quickly converted into cash.

acquisition costs Relates to historical transactions necessary to acquire a resource.

annual return on average investment Accounting method computed by dividing the average investment into the annual net earnings.

annual return on original investment Accounting method computed by dividing the original investment into the annual net earnings.

approximate rate of return See Accounting Method.

average book return on investment Accounting method computed by dividing the weighted average investment into the total net earnings less the original investment.

average return on average investment An accounting method dividing the sum of the average investment times the estimated depreciable life into the sums of the total net earnings less the original investment.

bail-out payback Another variation of the payback method which indicates what projects are a safer investment if it had to be abandoned including the salvage/scrap value of each investment proposal.

behavioral variables method Involves statistical analyses of variations in leadership ability correlated with increases in profits, productivity and other income factors.

benefit/cost analysis A ratio which measures the direct comparison of the present value benefits generated by a given investment with its costs.

book-value rate of return See Accounting Method.

capital employed Total assets less current liabilities.

cash flow Earnings after taxes plus depreciation.

cash-recovery period method See Payback Method.

compounding To what amount will $1.00 grow, if it earns r interest compounded for n periods.

controllable assets Consists of receivables and inventories of a sales territory.

cost approach Measures an investment in manpower similar to the capital expenditures investment concept.

GLOSSARY (Cont.)

cost of capital The average rate of earnings which investors require to induce them to provide all forms of long-term capital to the company.

cost reduction investments Investments where cost savings can be justified.

current ratio A general indicator of the ability of a company (borrower) to meet its current obligations.

day's sales on hand Indicates the average length in day's that inventories are held before sale.

day's sales outstanding Indication of the average age of net customer's accounts receivable.

debt-equity ratio Indicates the extent to which a company is financed by borrowed capital and the extent to which a company is financed by permanent contributed capital.

depreciation System of accounting which allocates the investment cost less salvage/scrap value over the estimated useful life of the asset, in a systematic or rational manner, in an effort of insuring investment recovery.

discounted cash flow Computes the rate of interest which equals the value of all future cash inflows attributable to the investment at a given point in time.

discounted payback method A variation of the payback method which uses discount factors.

discounting Shifts the value of money to be received in the future back to the present.

double-declining balance depreciation An accelerated method of depreciation computed by applying a fixed rate to the undepreciated balance at the end of each year.

economic approach Value of an employee is based on the marketplace.

economic values Present value of an individual in relation to the contribution to the future earnings of the organization.

excess present value index Uses net present values and expresses the results in the form of an index.

goodwill method Earnings in excess of an industry average would be calculated and then a proportion of this would be attributable to human factors.

gross profit to net sales Indicates the margin of sales over the cost of goods sold.

human assets to total assets A human asset investment ratio computed by dividing total assets into human assets.

human resource accounting The capitalizing of costs incurred in the training and future development of employees rather than expensing.

GLOSSARY (Cont.)

incremental cost of capital Any rate earned above the cost of financing is a favorable investment.

insurance value Value of an employee as to what amount a company is willing to insure an employee.

interest rate of return See Discounted Cash Flow.

investor's method See Discounted Cash Flow.

inventory turnover Indicates a company's turnover of inventory.

job earnings Calculation of MBO job value less the discounted cash flow of salary, training and related employee benefits.

leasing Contract whereby one party (lessor) conveys the use of a capital asset to another party (lessee) for a specified rate for a specified term of years.

lessee Party that receives the use of a capital asset.

lessor Party that conveys the use of a capital asset to another party.

MAPI A capital investment evaluation technique developed by the Machinery and Allied Products Institute and computed by taking the operating advantage, plus capital consumption avoided by the investment, minus capital consumption incurred, minus income tax adjustments, divided by the average net investment.

MBO job value Value of a job as measured through an MBO process.

maintaining current operations Projects essential to help the company continue and maintain its present position in the marketplace.

managing ratios Evaluates the various items of the balance sheet.

marginal efficiency of capital See Discounted Cash Flow.

marketing contribution Computed by taking net sales by marketing territory, less cost of goods sold of those products anticipated to be sold, less selling expenses held by the marketing territory to sell the product.

net earnings to net sales Measures the profitability of sales.

net earnings to net worth Ratio indicating how well the owners' capital is being employed in the business.

net earnings to total assets Ratio representing the return on funds invested in the company by both owners and creditors.

net present value See Discounted Cash Flow.

net sales to net working capital Indicates the activity of net working capital.

opportunity cost Measures the maximum yield from a specific investment that might have been earned if the investment had been applied to some alternative risk.

GLOSSARY (Cont.)

payback method   Measures the amount of time of a project's life in months and years, it takes to recoup from cash flows, the project's original investment.

payback period method   See Payback Method.

payback reciprocal   A variation of the payback method and is computed by dividing net cash flows by the investment.

payoff   See Payback Method.

payout   See Payback Method.

performance ratios   Reviews overall performance of a company as viewed by the outside community as a way of measuring current and potential performance.

present worth   See Discounted Cash Flow.

product growth and expansion investments   Projects relating to new facilities and new products, and expansion of existing plants and products.

profitability index   See Discounted Cash Flow.

profitability rate   Ratio which highlights the relationship of how much earnings are generated from a sales dollar. Computed by dividing net sales into net earnings.

profitability ratios   Relates to the earnings statement.

reciprocal   Reverse of compounding is discounting.

replacement costs   Estimated costs necessary today to replace a resource.

return on capital employed   Computed by dividing capital employed into net earnings.

return on controllable assets   Computed by dividing controllable assets into marketing contribution.

return on effort employed   A human resource evaluation technique which assigns point values.

return-on-investment   A financial tool which defines a problem, evaluates and weighs possible alternative investments, and brings into focus those qualitative factors affecting the decision which may not be expressed in quantitative terms.

return on total assets   A ratio computed by dividing total assets into net earnings.

sales to receivables   Indication of the turnover of receivables during a year.

salvage/scrap values   Value of an asset at the time of disposal or replacement.

scientific method   See Discounted Cash Flow.

selling expenses to net sales   Indicates the cost of selling a product.

straight-line depreciation   Allocates an equal portion of the investment over each period of use for the estimated life of the asset.

GLOSSARY (Cont.)

strategic investments Projects not capable of being measured.

sum-of-the-years'-digits depreciation An accelerated method of depreciation based on the sum of the digits for the estimated life of the asset.

time adjusted rate of return See Discounted Cash Flow.

turnover rate Reflects the rapidity with which capital committed to an operation is being worked. Computed by dividing the investment into net sales.

unadjusted rate of return See Accounting Method.

value approach Relates the value of the human resources as a function of the wages or profits of a company.

weighted average cost of capital Represents the composite weighted average of the rates for long-term debt, preferred stockholders' equity, and common stockholders' equity.

INDEX

HG
4028
C4
R255
1978

Rachlin, Robert, 1937–
  Return on investment :
strategies for profit